WHEN HEAVEN VISITS

Dramatic Accounts
of Military Heroes

ENDORSEMENTS

Combat is a unique and personal experience. Tests of faith and fear of failing are common. In these stories, Jerry has captured the essence of the experiences and has produced a great read.
—**Robert B. Flowers**, LTG General (Ret), US Army

Jerry Barnes's stories of the combat soldier are vivid, touching, and real. They are "must read" accounts of the battlefield experience.
—**Betsy Ashton**, author of *The Mad Max Mystery Series—Unsafe Haven, Uncharted Territory,* and *Unintended Consequences*

Jerry Barnes has brilliantly pulled together a magnificent collection of personal accounts by ordinary, yet heroic, men and women who humbly recount acts that we all can greatly appreciate and strive to emulate. Take your time to read and appreciate the powerful and touching nature of these recollections and feel the emotions of everyday Americans who, yes, fit the very accurate description of "heroes" as they serve their country on the battlefield.
—**Don T. Riley**, MG (Ret), US Army

I have been tracking the writing progress of this treasured friend. His heart for sharing the heroic stories of combat veterans is genuine, compelling, and inspiring.
—**John Peabody**, MG, (Ret), US Army

These stories must be told, and Barnes's superb writing style allows the reader to feel a part of each special heroic moment. Our veterans face unbelievable challenges, make decisive, life-and-death decisions, and survive extraordinary odds, feeling God's presence as their fates unfold.
—**Gary J. Cummins**, Lt Col, (Ret), US Marine Corps

Jerry serves on the board of FRAME, a nonprofit serving homeless and disabled veterans and their families. We are counting the days until this revealing, action-packed book is published.

—**Lisa Sibitzky**, President of FRAME (Family Readiness and Military Ease), Roanoke, Virginia

WHEN HEAVEN VISITS

Dramatic Accounts of
Military Heroes

Twenty-Four Stories of Military Service
As Retold by Jerry Barnes, Man of Faith, Former Soldier, and Engineer

PUBLISHING THE POSITIVE
ELK LAKE PUBLISHING INC.
Plymouth, Massachusetts

Cover and Interior Design: Derinda Babcock

Editor(s): Andrea L. Hitefield, Deb Haggerty

Author Represented by the Steve Laube Agency

PUBLISHED BY: Elk Lake Publishing, Inc., 35 Dogwood Dr., Plymouth, MA 02360, 2019

Library Cataloging Data

Names: Barnes, Jerry (Jerry Barnes)

When Heaven Visits: Dramatic Accounts of Military Heroes / Jerry Barnes

132 p. 23cm × 15cm (9in × 6 in.)

Description: Stories of war, told to the author by those who were there.

Identifiers: ISBN-13: 978-1-950051-51-9 (trade hardcover)| 978-1-950051-24-3 (trade paperback) | 978-1-950051-25-0 (POD) | 978-1-950051-26-7 (e-book.)

Key Words: Armed Services, War, Miracles, Army, Marines, Survival

LCCN: 2019937781 Nonfiction

DEDICATION

I would like to dedicate this book to the loving memory of my mother, Allie Mae Barnes, who talked in "stories" and gave me a genuine love for story-telling and writing.

CONTENTS

FOREWORD

Combat duty has many impacts, often traumatic, on veterans. It leaves them with both physical and emotional scars. Many of their injuries can be treated as they allow God's healing to occur. Some disabilities, such as loss of limbs, sight, and hearing are more challenging to cope with, but the mental and emotional scars are what may have lasting effects. Unfortunately, all of these injuries are the reality of war.

PTSD (Post Traumatic Stress Disorder) is a common problem for those who have served in combat. Veterans with PTSD become anxious and even angry without cause. They are plagued with flashbacks and have a hard time sleeping or relaxing. Other symptoms include depression, panic attacks, and a state of constant alertness. These individuals have the most difficulty with recovery, especially after witnessing and experiencing the horrors of war. Several of the heroes in *When Heaven Visits* suffer from PTSD.

Some veterans are diagnosed before leaving military service while others show symptoms afterward. This disorder partially disables the individual, which allows him (or her) to receive medical treatment and other services through the VA (Veteran Affairs). Some people suffering with PTSD deny they have the condition and are either uninformed or too proud to seek help, even though assistance is readily available. I would like to encourage anyone who identifies with the veterans in this book, and has not sought help, to do so.

PREFACE

"So help me God" are the last four words in the oath of enlistment to the US Armed Services. When I repeated them many years ago, I gave little thought to what they might mean in the future. At that point, they simply represented a "matter of fact" commitment to serve my country. No doubt, most of the young men and women featured in this book had similar reactions in the beginning. Some of them clearly experienced God's divine help in the midst of combat. In a few of these stories, God's divine intervention spared their lives.

Perhaps another part of the oath presented inductees with even greater reason for thought, "… to protect and defend the Constitution of the United States against all enemies, foreign and domestic." *What might this commitment require of them*? For some, it would mean losing fellow comrades in action. Others would have close calls with death themselves or sustain injuries that would follow them through life. But for all soldiers who faced combat, it would mean putting their lives on the line daily to preserve peace in the Middle East, fight for human rights around the globe, and ensure the continued freedom of their own country and loved ones back home.

ACKNOWLEDGMENTS

A special thanks to my wife, Laura, for her help and dedication in making this book a reality. I am also grateful to Andrea Hitefield, who worked tirelessly editing, correcting, and assembling the manuscript, and to Pam Hardenbrook, who edited for me until she had to move her household.

The idea for this book came from long time literary agent, Les Stobbe, who asked at our first meeting, "Are you a veteran?" That question led me to seek out veterans with near death encounters who were willing to share their stories. Thank you, Les, for encouraging me in this adventure and leading me to some of America's best!

I am especially grateful to Deb Haggerty of Elk Lake Publishing, Inc. for believing in the potential of the book and offering me the opportunity to publish *When Heaven Visits*.

INTRODUCTION

When enlistees first become members of the US Armed Services, they are normally young and full of energy, potential, and hope. No one thinks about the possibility of being injured or killed while in military service. Most have other objectives, such as help with their education, developing a life skill, health and retirement benefits, VA benefits, or potentially to make the service a career. Sadly, a few become casualties of war. This book describes some of the less desirable aspects of being in a combat zone.

I chose the title, *When Heaven Visits*, to call the reader's attention to the role God played in helping these soldiers get through the tough situations they faced, whether in battle or at another time relative to their military service. Nothing except divine intervention can explain why the rocket-propelled grenades took a ninety-degree dive into the ground just before they reached Albert, or how an unexplained voice guided Chris in his escape from a burning vehicle. Each of these veterans had a story to share which clearly revealed how God had either protected them in the midst of combat or led them out of the path of danger.

As the saying goes, "There are no atheists in foxholes." Some people have to go through a near-death experience to make them realize their dependence on the Lord. Surely, those soldiers who have encountered the angels of God on the battlefield can never dispute his existence. I will be forever grateful for his intervention in my own life. He kept me from being in a helicopter that went down in Vietnam killing all but one of the occupants.

THE AMBUSH

RYAN'S STORY

The Lord is my strength and my shield; my heart trusted in him, and I am helped; therefore my heart greatly rejoices, and with my song, I praise him. (Psalm 28:7)

As our Isuzu Trooper came around a bend in the road, we encountered a maroon sedan blocking the roadway. Four Al Qaeda operatives, with black scarves around their heads, stood around the vehicle pointing AK-47 automatic weapons directly at us. A white car sped up behind us with four more Al Qaeda occupants, also hoisting weapons in our direction. An almost overwhelming terror consumed me. *We were going to die.* My next thoughts came quickly, *Show us how to escape, Lord. But if this is the end ... please make it quick.*

I yelled to Bazzi, "Don't stop for any reason! Drive as fast as you can!" He hit the gas as the white car approached from the left side. The enemy began firing on us simultaneously from the left and the front. We were caught in a planned, crossfire ambush.

As members of a special operations unit, one of many operating in Iraq, we spent months training for these types of missions. In our world, mission failure was not an option.

Earlier in the day, around noon, we left Ramadi for a routine mission to Lake Tartar, about an hour away. Bazzi, an Iraqi loyalist and contract employee, drove our Isuzu Trooper. Our goal that rainy day was to gather useful information on a high-value target. Did he travel alone or with security? We believed such a valuable leader wouldn't be alone and expected to see a trail car. While planning the mission, we identified the target's mobile device and isolated the exact days and times he normally made calls. During those calls, we could lock in on the phone's coordinate location within a few feet.

Our main objective was to find and identify the target, determine the number of people with him, access how they were armed, and evaluate the potential for capturing him. A secondary goal was to evaluate the possibility of air support and follow him. The final objective was to judge whether we should snag him then or later. We also had command authority to eliminate him if he resisted capture or ran (became a "squirter").

Two previous attempts to locate him had proven unsuccessful, but this day differed for several reasons. First, it was Friday—mosque day for the Muslim faith (similar to Sunday for Christians). Secondly, rain came pouring down with temperatures alternating between fifty and sixty degrees in the daytime and falling below freezing at night. Because of the terrible weather, we initially considered aborting the mission.

Bazzi drove, while I sat beside him in the front seat. Lance and Dean sat in the middle seat. After arriving in the reconnaissance zone, we drove around for more than two hours in the rain. Looking back, we should have noticed the unusually few cars on the road and so many people walking in the rain. After being in the target's suspected area of operation for hours with no sightings, we decided we should head back to base before nightfall.

That's when things changed. We received an alert from base. The target's phone was active. They gave us a ten-digit grid which Lance quickly plugged into his computer, and then exclaimed, "We just drove by there a few minutes ago." Bazzi turned around and headed north again, traveling along the canal.

We spotted our target on the canal's east side crouched in weeds, yet still visible behind a small wooden guard rail, using his satellite phone. We drove past him and turned the corner. We expected to see a security detail around him, but surprisingly found him alone. In retrospect, I wish things hadn't happened as they did.

We contacted our Task Force Commander, explained the situation, and received authority to snag and detain the individual. The target was approximately fifteen yards from us when we exited our vehicle and began walking south, in a V-formation along the canal. Bazzi stayed in the Trooper, backing the vehicle as we walked.

As we neared the target, he raised his hands in the air and stood facing us. We motioned for him to lift his shirt, so we could check for explosives.

But when we spoke in English, his whole demeanor changed. He began yelling "La-La-La-La," and took off running. When he reached the canal, he jumped off the edge of the steep embankment.

Dean returned to the Trooper, ensuring Bazzi wouldn't spook and run.

Lance and I looked over the fifteen-foot drop to the waterway. The target held onto branches at the bottom of the bank and moved from branch to branch along the canal. Lance and I started firing. People emerged from a shack on the other side of the canal yelling Arabic obscenities. The target jumped into the water and began swimming towards them. But before he reached the far shore, we had a clear shot and took him out.

After doing a quick search for the terrorist's phone, we ran back to the Trooper and headed south to Ramadi. Although no visible traffic followed us, we were confident the enemy would communicate with others in the nearby area, alerting them to be on the lookout for a white Trooper with three Americans, driven by an Iraqi loyalist.

We were not surprised when the incident happened. Trained to anticipate some type of ambush, we did what we could to prepare for the inevitable. Dean crawled into the back seat of the Trooper, facing the rear for visibility from that direction. Lance took the left side, and I covered the front of the Trooper. Between us, we could cover one hundred eighty degrees of firing circumference. Two cars, one white and the other dark maroon, approached us from the north, coming close enough to identify our vehicle, and then backed off a significant distance. The maroon Opel approached a second time. No guns were in sight, so Bazzi kept driving the speed limit as the car passed us. The Opel's four occupants looked directly at the four of us, sped up significantly, and drove out of sight. When we navigated a curve to the right, the maroon Opel was blocking the roadway, and the white car approached from the rear a second time. We were targets in a planned ambush. Terrified for our lives, and seeing no way out, I prayed.

Caught in a crossfire, Dean, Lance, and I began returning fire from our respective positions inside the Trooper. I leaned out the right front window, firing on the four men from the maroon sedan, while Lance and Dean began firing on the occupants of the white car encroaching on the left side of our vehicle. When Bazzi sped up to pass the vehicle blocking the roadway, he ran over one of the bad guys and clipped the front bumper of the maroon sedan. During the firefight with the white car, Lance did something uncommonly selfless and heroic, which saved our lives. Responding to his military instinct and experience and his own sheer courage, he diverted his eyes from the gunman most threatening his own life to intentionally shoot the driver of the white car. In so doing, the white car sped out of control, ran off the road and crashed into a ditch. Sadly, Lance took a bullet to the head and was killed while performing this heroic deed.

During the exchange, I received a shot through the skull, slightly damaging the left parietal lobe. The bullet exited the left side through the front—above my left eye and approximately three inches from its entry of the skull—causing me to temporarily black out. I was hanging out the right window at the time. Miraculously, my rifle sling caught on the right front mirror, preventing me from falling from the vehicle.

Dean received two gruesome shots. A 7.62 mm round penetrated his right shin blowing a three-inch hole out the back of his leg. A second round penetrated the thigh of his same leg. He suffered severe blood loss. When I regained consciousness and assessed the situation, I crawled back to Lance. I felt totally helpless—he was gone. Then I moved to the rear seat occupied by Dean. I helped him get up from the floor of the vehicle, applied a tourniquet to stop the bleeding, and offered him a morphine shot. He refused despite the pain and kept his weapon pointed, ready to continue firing. We changed magazines in his weapon and determined a quick plan for dealing with another ambush. I asked him, "Can you shoot?"

"Yes," he replied, "I can shoot."

While the Trooper cleared the ambush, our left front tire was flat and the engine sputtered. We drove down the highway slowly as I called Headquarters and spoke with our commander. He immediately launched the QRF (Quick Reaction Force) and advised it was an hour away. The blood from my wound soaked the iPhone and gummed up the speakers, making it difficult to hear what he said.

I noticed two cars maneuvering at a gas station just up the road. At this point, we reasonably assumed everyone was the enemy. Two vehicles approached our Trooper from the north and south exits of the gas station. Dean got ready to shoot, but I told Bazzi, "Just stay on the road and go past them." I leaned out of the window as we went past the gas station's first exit. One of the cars pulled in behind us. Dean dumped a whole magazine into the car's windshield. I grabbed Bazzi's AK-47, which had an even bigger round than Dean's weapon. As we passed the south exit, a second vehicle pulled in behind us. From the window of the Trooper, I unloaded a full magazine into the windshield of that vehicle. We took out both vehicles.

The Trooper was on three wheels, and Bazzi, wound tight, drove too fast as we approached another intersection. Bazzi hit the brakes. The Trooper spun around in the road and landed in a ditch. Bazzi and I jumped out and stood with loaded weapons pointed up the road. I looked over at Bazzi, still shaking, "We're in a bad spot." I told him. "If they get us, they are going to be harder on you than Dean and me."

He nodded. "We can't go alive."

It was quiet outside and getting dark as we watched down the road for a vehicle to approach. We pulled Dean from the Trooper and hid him in a potato field behind the vehicle with his weapon, a radio, and a strobe light in hand. "Don't make a sound," I said. "If they get us, they won't get you."

Dusk had settled in. We tried to adjust to night operations with inadequate lighting—a significant planning flaw on my part.

I told Bazzi to go flag down a car. When a vehicle approached, I ran to it, put an AK47 in the driver's face and yelled, "Push us out of the ditch!" With that kind of encouragement, the three guys in the car didn't take long to get the Trooper back on the road. They were all frightened and unarmed, but we ordered them to lie face down in a nearby ditch until we departed. Bazzi and I put Dean back in the Trooper and drove away. Clearly rattled, he tried to go west rather than south. I said, "If we go that way the QRF won't be able to find us. They are going to be looking for us heading east toward the base." But Bazzi feared a third ambush ahead of us. He had good reason to be scared—he had listened to the conversations of the guys who pushed us out of the ditch. Bazzi told me later, "They were almost certainly terrorists themselves, but showed no interest in finishing us off."

Approximately a mile or so up the road stood three lighted houses about a hundred and fifty feet off the road. As we passed, the lights went out and occupants within began firing at us. Since we were approaching a bridge, a thought raced through my mind: *that's a signal. Someone's on the bridge. They're gonna detonate an IED.* I looked for someone on the ridgeline with a detonating device. Not seeing anyone, we crossed the bridge cautiously, but without incident, and approached the entrance to the main highway.

Shortly after entering the interstate, the Trooper died finally died. We decided to commandeer a private vehicle to take us back to Ramadi. This strategy seemed simple but proved difficult. Cars passed our disabled Trooper at sixty to seventy miles per hour, while Bazzi and I tried unsuccessfully to flag them down. Finally, a car slowed to pass our stranded vehicle. Bazzi waved and I pointed a weapon in his direction to further encourage him to stop. The driver, a school teacher, drove a vehicle too small to fit all of us. So, we loaded Dean and Bazzi into his car and sent them to find help.

I removed Lance from the Trooper, took all weapons, ammo, communications, and signaling devices and relocated to the bottom of a ditch below the interstate. About forty-five minutes passed with no contact from anyone. I walked back to the road several times, thinking about country roads in rural Oklahoma and wondering if we would make it back. With visions of home, I asked God to help Dean and Bazzi get to the check point safely. Assuming they found help, a lot of people were probably looking for Lance and me.

The roar of a Humvee had never sounded so wonderful. Bazzi, Dean, and the teacher made the checkpoint successfully. Base dispatched a team of rescue personnel to search for Lance and me. Bazzi even returned with them, saying, "We started the day together, and we will end it together."

When I arrived back at the checkpoint, a medic asked me, "Were you hit?"

"I don't think so."

"You have skull fragments and tissue all over you, a bullet wound in your head, and an exit wound to prove you are wrong!"

****

The doctors decided Dean and I needed immediate medical evacuation. I woke up in Germany with a tube surgically inserted into my head. A few hours later, I was evacuated to Andrews Air Force Base in DC. After debriefing, I moved to Bethesda Hospital and saw the kickoff for the 2006 Super Bowl, when the Steelers played the Seahawks.

During the investigation, there were comments about being a cowboy, which lasted for a couple of days. In the end, General Stanley McCrystal shut such unfounded accusations down pretty quickly. I received a Silver Star and a Purple Heart. They wanted to do an award ceremony, but I didn't want any part of that for a failed mission in which one of my buddies lost his life.

What I want everyone who reads this to remember is that Dean and I are still alive only because of God's protective care and Lance's overwhelming heroism. I see his selfless actions to save his friends as the most memorable part of the entire mission. I will always be indebted to his memory and grateful for what he did for us. "Greater love has no one than this, than to lay down one's life for his friends" (John 15:13).

SHOCKING NEWS

> Let each of you look not only for his own interests but also for
> the interests of others. (Phil 2:4)

A helicopter with seven US soldiers was shot down yesterday near
Pleiku, in the Central Highlands of Vietnam. There was one survivor among
those on board the downed craft. In addition to the commander, an army
colonel, those also killed included two officers, two pilots, and one enlisted
man. All deceased soldiers came from various US Army units operating
in this volatile region of Vietnam. Early reports indicate the aircraft was
brought down by hostile enemy fire from the North Vietnamese Army.

This notification of Corps of Engineers' losses during the Vietnam
War was one of many announcements of US casualties during the conflict.
However, this one was personal, hit me like a baseball bat to the chest, and
caused my knees to weaken.

The memorial service occurred two weeks later. My wife and I paid our
respects to Col. Adams's wife and family and sat in the back of the packed
Episcopal Church. During the service, grieving was subdued and remarks
respectful, as Col. Adams would have liked. Comments touched on all the
appropriate themes: love of God, family, country, and the cost of freedom.
No one spoke words second-guessing the US decision to be in Vietnam.
Neither the colonel nor his family would have wanted such words. In the
front row, his son, an army lieutenant, sat beside his grieving mother.

The colonel's wife was a teacher in our daughter's daycare center in the
Episcopal Church. Our daughter adored her. There was never a day she

didn't jump out of the car and receive a hug from Mrs. Adams. It was like having grandma in her daycare.

Laura and I sat near the back of the packed church. Trying to be attentive to the words, I found myself gazing at the floor and thinking about a conversation Colonel Adams and I shared three months earlier.

When I appeared in the doorway of his office and saluted, the boss returned the salute and immediately stood up and walked towards me with his hand outstretched. "Hi, Jerry," he greeted me (never lieutenant—he always called subordinates by their first names). "What brings you to see me today?"

"Well, sir, Laura and I have both talked and prayed about this, and we have decided for me to volunteer and go with you—if you would allow me—and serve with you in Vietnam. Perhaps you would permit me to be your aide. If memory serves me, you are a couple of months ahead of me in time served here in Norfolk. My hope is for you to contact the army's assignments desk for lieutenants and ask them to send me orders now so I could accompany you."

As he took his seat, he smiled and said warmly, "Your offer honors me, Jerry. It honors me that you would say that. Are you sure?"

"Yes, sir. Absolutely," I answered.

"Do you plan to make the Army a career?"

"No, sir. I have an offer from the Virginia Department of Highways to enter their training program when discharged from the army."

The colonel looked me in the eyes, and then turned around and looked out of his window for fifteen to twenty seconds. That pause, and his thought process, likely saved my life.

As he turned around and faced me, he remarked, "Again, I am truly honored to have someone offer what you have. If you were going to stay in the army, I would accept your offer and contact the lieutenant's assignment desk on your behalf. It is a little strange the army has not given you orders already since you are so close to beginning your final year of service. I know the president has withdrawn troops from Vietnam. He just announced a few weeks back that fifty thousand personnel would be leaving the Vietnam Theater and returning to duty stations elsewhere. The word is he'll continue that policy of disengagement. Who knows, perhaps you won't get orders to Vietnam at all. You may be able to complete your tour of duty here in

Norfolk. But if you do get a call concerning orders before I leave, stop back in and I will request a change to the brigade I'm commanding."

I thanked him, saluted, and left his office.

We sat quietly during the service for Colonel Adams and left at the conclusion with somber feelings. One thought kept running through my mind: *He saved my life. He saved my life.*

Laura and I completed our tour in Norfolk and left the army three years to the date of entry into active duty.

Col. Carroll E. Adams was promoted—posthumously—to Brigadier General. He was one of two Corps of Engineers General Officers killed in the Vietnam War.

THE LONG ROAD TO RECOVERY

KEVIN'S STORY

> The Lord bless you and keep you; the Lord make his face shine upon you, and be gracious to you; the Lord lift up his countenance upon you, and give you peace. (Numbers 6:24-26)

You can be injured in combat and not even realize how seriously. Fortunately, despite my injuries, I lived to tell about it.

Two soldiers and I sat in the front vehicle, fifty yards ahead of the second Humvee, when it happened. Operating the fifty-caliber turret, I heard—but never saw—the blast. I never felt the pieces of metal shrapnel penetrate my metal helmet, break the right side of my protective glasses and embed themselves into my right eye socket. I fell to the floor of the turret, touched my eye socket and felt the broken glasses. Blood covered the right side of my face and soaked the front of my uniform. I applied a bandage from my medical kit to stop the bleeding. These actions occurred simultaneously as a sort of delayed reaction following the blast. Even with the blood running down my face, I felt no pain—perhaps my adrenalin had kicked in.

Consistent with army protocol for vehicles caught in a blast, our Humvee quickly sped two hundred yards away from the blast area to avoid the possibility of a trap meant to entice us into a killing zone. With every tire on our vehicle flattened by shrapnel, we crossed a small hill and stopped. Seeing no sign of a trap, we returned to the blast area. A massive plume of smoke arose into view as we crested the hill. Below us, smoke and flames engulfed our buddies' Humvee. My stomach dropped, *Oh God— no! All three of my friends are dead, and I am alone!*

I shuddered with dread as we moved closer to their vehicle. "They're alive!" I screamed in full euphoria and rushed toward them as two of my buddies struggled to get Chris from his machine gun turret and away from the burning vehicle. Shane and I pulled security to protect them, but by the grace of God, the enemy had already gone.

Special forces medics performed emergency treatment on all of our injuries and re-bandaged my eye. I couldn't see anything when they removed the first bandage. "Do I have a right eye?" I asked. Both Shane and the medic assured me the eye was intact, but the eyelid was damaged badly. Shane even cracked a joke about how I looked. We had no idea how severe our injuries were at that point. A half hour after the explosion, I still felt virtually no pain.

I underwent the first of four surgeries to repair my badly torn eyelid at the medical facility in Mosul. After locating shrapnel in the upper part of my eye socket, my doctors decided to evacuate me to Ballad, Kuwait, where they had an eye specialist on staff. Medical personnel in both Mosul and Kuwait discussed the uncertainties surrounding treatment for my eye injury (particularly given the vexing problem of embedded shrapnel).

A wide range of emotions crossed my mind as tears filled my eyes: *Am I going to lose my sight? What will my family think? What does the future hold now?*

Since everything happened so fast, my battle brothers kept my family updated with news about my progress. My wife, Beth, received word of my eye injury before I could even call her.

The brotherhood between soldiers in a battle zone is incredible, yet difficult to describe. We all foreknew we would be willing to risk our own lives to save a "battle brother." Because of that special bond, I didn't want to leave them. While being treated in Kuwait, I realized, "I didn't even get to say goodbye."

I found some comfort in learning the army planned to evacuate Chris to Kuwait as well. Doctors in Mosul were unable to treat the serious shrapnel damage to his legs, arms, and face. I had been in Kuwait for a couple of days before Chris arrived on the scene.

Here I had my second surgery to patch the torn eyelid. Having done all they could do in Kuwait, they finally decided to evacuate me to Walter Reed Army Medical Center for further treatments. Injured soldiers were first flown to Germany before being transported to Walter Reed. The doctor gave me a shot to help me rest and endure the eight-hour flight from Germany to Washington. I had only been there for a day when Chris joined me.

The early treatment plan in Walter Reed involved a great many eye drops to the right eye over a period of six to eight weeks and frequent monitoring of pressure levels in the eye. Doctors believed my sight would gradually return, so we all waited for encouraging signs.

The doctors decided to postpone a long-term treatment plan for the shrapnel embedded in my right eye. Since I experienced little or no pain, the shrapnel was not a major concern. My greatest concern was not being able to see anything except streams of light. They administered a regimen of pain meds and eye drops during my convalescence.

But thirty days later, I still had no vision, and there was a lot of pressure in my eye. The doctors realized something was seriously wrong. Pressure in my eye should have been diminishing, yet remained extremely high. The doctors performed a third surgery to remove blood particles from my eye socket, repair the tear ducts in my retina, and remove cataracts that had formed due to trauma from the injury.

Over the next few months, some sight finally began to return and the pressure in my eye began dropping. A fourth surgery repaired my drooping eyelids. After two years, my vision has improved somewhat. A fifth surgery is being discussed to deal with glaucoma and to put a shunt in the eye for drainage. I am passing on that at the moment, because it could create new problems and even cause me to lose my sight completely. So, for now, my vision is not excellent but passable at 20/150. I am dealing with the reality of carrying this injury for the rest of my life. I have accepted the adjustment to a "new norm." I use drops five times per day and may eventually need to have the shunt surgery. I also accept that shrapnel will almost certainly be in my eye socket for the rest of my life.

Let me close with an incident that sums up how Beth and I both feel about the future. When I arrived at Walter Reed from Germany, Beth came up to see me. We knew we faced an uncertain future. We had just spoken with the doctor who apologized because he couldn't give me a more positive outlook as he described what we faced. We just sat there looking at each other, and Beth started to cry.

"What's wrong?" I asked.

Her response sums up exactly how we both feel. "I was just looking at a young man who is a triple amputee and thinking how fortunate we are."

*******★★★★★★★★*****

The US has excellent medical care for soldiers: available emergency field care from terrific medics, hospitals in Mosul and Ballad, Kuwait, a large military hospital in Germany, and of course several hospitals in the US—Walter Reed among them.

The financial sacrifice of police families in the Roanoke area deserves special mention as well. They sacrificed to help me and my family with travel and lodging expenses during my treatments and convalescence in DC.

THE EXPLOSION

So you shall rejoice in every good thing which the Lord your
God has given to you and your house. (Deuteronomy 26:11a)

A glowing tracer whizzed by my helmet, barely missing my right ear.
On my first combat patrol, this welcome wagon to Tal Afar—the "Wild
West of Iraq"—provided a startling, lasting memory. Our unit of Virginia
army reservists, called to one year of active duty, was embedded with active
duty special forces—also assigned to this hell hole. The combined unit
patrolled and fought thirty miles north of Mosul.

My police job back home provided ample opportunity to experience
dangerous situations—or so I thought. Accidents, shootings, and suicides
didn't surprise me. Yet, thirteen years of police experience did little to
prepare me for the carnage I saw in Iraq. I never witnessed small children,
shot in the legs, placed in the middle of a road to slow convoy traffic and
provide staging for a surprise Al Qaeda attack—until Iraq. I never saw a
leg and foot with the shoe still attached fall from the back of an emergency
ambulance. Until Iraq, I had never baked in 120° heat, adorned in a stylish
metal helmet, wearing seventy pounds of body armor, and carrying a rifle.
I experienced all of these, as well as a bullet coming within inches of my
head, during my first two weeks in Tal Afar.

The most action I'd experienced in twelve years of reserve duty was two
weeks of training at Fort Jackson, breaking in raw recruits to the joys of
being in the army. As a part of Virginia's 80th Division, a training unit, we
expected a logistics supply mission, but never engaging in actual combat. I
comforted myself, family, and friends by telling them, "Logistics is nothing
more than a back channel, rear echelon duty, far away from real action."

I was badly mistaken.

That first mission seemed simple enough—team up with special forces and secure a polling site on Route Reno, near the Village of Muhallabia, twenty miles from Fort Tal Afar. US elections are generally a one-day, ho-hum event where people calmly drive to a polling place, stand in line, and cast their vote. We assumed this one would be similar.

Elections to select 275 members to the Iraqi Council of Representatives were held on December 15, 2005, complete with distinctive purple fingertips signifying, "I voted today." In Iraq, this historic event was the first view of democracy many Iraqi citizens ever witnessed.

On December 10th, our unit received the mission to prepare and secure the polling site near our forward operating base. Polling site security became a matter of urgent concern. The Iraqi population needed reassurance of their personal safety and security to vote. We loaded our armored Humvees with food, water, and sleeping bags. Watchful in all directions, the two-vehicle convoy traveled at a deliberate pace toward the polling site. We saw recent craters in the roadway, some three to five feet deep, caused by improvised explosive devices (IEDs). Chris, another reservist, was concerned as we passed one of the craters. He'd barely survived an earlier explosion which created that one. He relived the event and told us how he had placed two tourniquets on the driver's leg to save his life.

Impressions in the craters confirmed what we learned in the pre-departure briefing: the bad guys didn't like the idea of people voting and seemed determined to disrupt the event. Such visible evidence reconfirmed my fear-filled impressions from my first two weeks in Iraq. Never take anything for granted. Never relax vigilance or you could find yourself, without warning, dead.

After we established our staging room in a school building which became the polling site, we needed more supplies, particularly concertina wire for perimeter security. Both vehicles headed back to the fort with special forces in the lead. We loaded and secured the additional supplies and hastily departed for the return trip. Our special forces' vehicle, a football field ahead of us, contained Dan, Doug, and Kevin. My Humvee contained all Virginia policemen: I drove, Chapman (Chappy) rode shotgun and secured the vehicle's right side, and Chris sat in the 50-caliber machine gun turret.

Along the way, my mind dreamed of home and fondly recalled that today was my son's third birthday. I thought of the call I would make to him later—the highlight of my day. About twelve miles down the road, the lead vehicle turned right at Checkpoint 99 where civilian traffic had pulled off to allow our two-vehicle convoy to pass. Just before I turned, a white taxi with orange bumpers pulled beside our vehicle. When Chris saw the driver's somber expression, he recognized it was a trap and fired his 9mm pistol. At that point, I connected the dots in my mind—our vehicle was the primary target for a massive roadside bomb. The taxi exploded with a gigantic *BOOM*—heard three miles away—and generated an enormous fireball.

Blood rapidly flowed from my right eye, blinding me. A feeling of panic overwhelmed me as I saw the Humvee's hood erupt into flames. A rhythmic, excruciating pain pulsated in my head, and our vehicle filled with smoke. Fire surrounded us. Chappy yelled, "Gun it!" But with the steering wheel bent sideways, there was nothing to gun. I felt for my legs to see if they were still attached. My eyes didn't focus, but my hands instinctively opened the door. I could feel the scorched roadway burning underneath my boots. Somehow, Chappy emerged in front of me. We started to run, but then saw Chris still in the burning vehicle struggling to exit. Shrapnel had wounded his face and arms and severed an artery. He bled profusely. Compounding the danger, extra ammunition was "cooking off" in the cab and rear of the Humvee. And Chris had a pistol in his hand and his vest loaded with grenades.

We finally pulled Chris from the vehicle, but he immediately fell on the burning roadway. Chappy and I grabbed him by the back of his vest and pulled him to safety with him screaming, "My body is on fire!"

With our hands, we hysterically beat out the flames on his clothing. Chappy placed a tourniquet on Chris's arm to stop the bleeding but the rest of our first aid was in the burning Humvee. That Humvee, still filled with explosives and in flames, sat close to us. Too close. We had to move. But we were in the desert, alone and wounded.

I grabbed my rifle and tried to secure the area with my one good eye while Chappy feverishly worked on Chris. Mercifully, I made radio contact with G Troop of the Third Armored Cavalry Regiment, who heard the explosion and raced to assist. Our lead vehicle with special forces Dan, Doug, and Kevin had also sustained damage from the explosion but no major injuries. They joined us, traveling on four flat tires, at about the same time as the special forces with the medics and the armored cavalry arrived on the scene. Kevin, a Virginia guy wearing an eye bandage, walked up to me and asked, "Is my eye still there? I think it's gone." I peeked at him with my good eye and saw that his bleeding eyelid seemed inside out. I told him to calm down, flip his eyelid, and he would survive. Later, Kevin learned he had shrapnel in the back of his eye socket causing significant damage to his eye. When I look back, this conversation seemed kind of funny in the middle of a life-threatening situation. Only a close brotherhood of GIs could find a bit of humor in the midst of combat and chaos. Our laughter soon turned to tears, and feelings of hate towards Iraq and the war that brought us here.

Slightly more conscious now, I stumbled over to Doug and asked for a bandage for my eye. Chris and Chappy lay on the ground. "Lie down, Shane," Chappy said. "Put your head on my leg until your wounds are treated." I didn't know whether to cry or puke.

When another special forces team of medics showed up, I asked, "Is my injured eye in the socket and intact?" The medic examined my eye then spoke in a distinctive southern drawl, "Well, you'll be OK, but you won't win any beauty contests for a while."

When I asked about Chappy, another medic replied, "He's having a hard time breathing, and has a nice goose egg between his eyes. But he'll be OK."

A Bradley fighting vehicle came and took all three of us to the landing zone for a medivac to Mosul. We walked into the hospital together, refusing stretchers. Chris, the most severely injured, immediately went into surgery to fix his arm and a wound on his face. His injuries eventually required evacuation to Germany. Chappy received treatment for smoke inhalation and significant bumps and bruises. I had a couple of stitches put in my torn eyelid then got a good luck pat on the back. Chappy and I returned to duty the next morning.

The 3rd ACR guys said the blast was equivalent to seven or eight 155 artillery rounds exploding at once. A single 155 round is filled with approximately twenty-five pounds of dynamite and weighs about a hundred pounds. Seven of them exploding simultaneously explained two things. One, it clarified why the white taxi only had the transmission and drive shaft remaining at the site. Second, it revealed the strength of the Humvee's armor. The vehicle's ability to sustain a large explosive event from a distance of five feet yet protect three occupants was truly amazing. To me, it was simply a testament to great armor protection and God's providence that saved three GI lives.

Shane received a Purple Heart and Army Commendation Medal for Valor.

TEN MINUTES TO LIVE

DONNIE'S STORY

For it is written: 'He shall give his angels charge over you, to keep you.' (Luke 4:10)

Donnie stuffed two extra pairs of socks and his well-worn Auburn Tiger shirt into a blue air force duffel bag. After checking his bulging bag for the ticket purchased two months earlier, he threw it over his shoulder and headed to a train station near his London apartment. His long awaited thirty-day Christmas vacation was finally beginning. It was December 21, 1988.

Donnie and his blue bag occupied two seats on the train. His watch read four hours until "wheels up." Confident in his impeccable sense of timing, Donnie thought, *This early, I'll beat the rush through check-in and be at the gate at least two hours early*. It was sure to be a smooth trip to Houston.

Donnie would not have been so confident if he had known that not a single one of the 243 passengers, nor the crew of sixteen who boarded Pan Am Flight 103 that fateful day, would be alive seven hours later.

The train lumbered along as Donnie thought about his time in the air force with his best friend "Wild Bill." Bill had left the air force to return home to the Lone Star State. But Donnie, a "lifer," continued his career as a base security policeman.

He looked at his watch again. In less than ten hours, Bill would meet him in Houston's Hobby Airport terminal. *Let the fun begin!* He smiled.

Donnie entered Heathrow Airport and groaned. Seven people were already in line to check in for Pan Am Flight 103. It was 2:31 in the afternoon; the airplane was not scheduled to depart until 6:25. *I shouldn't be surprised, it is Christmas, and everyone is heading home for the holidays.*

Donnie took the eighth place in line and dropped his heavy blue bag. Forty minutes later, he was pleading his case to the Pan Am attendant: "Ma'am, I have never had to produce a passport for commercial travel in the past. My military ID has always been sufficient."

"It would be sufficient this time if you were in uniform, but you're not. You need a passport to board any international Pan Am flight. Is there a way for you to get your passport and return to the gate?"

Donnie glanced at his watch, "Maybe, but it will be a rush."

"Well, if it would help, you can leave your bag here while you get your passport. You don't have to wait in line a second time. Just come directly to me. I'll check your passport *and* your bag."

Donnie left Heathrow and raced back to the train. Less than three hours remained for him to return to his apartment, grab his passport, show it to the sympathetic Pan Am gate agent, check his bag, and get to the departing gate in time to board the flight.

Sometimes, unexplained "angels of mercy" watch over us. One surely watched over Donnie that day.

He made it home, grabbed his passport, raced back to Heathrow, found the boarding agent, and showed her his passport. "Grab your bag and come with me," she said. "I've already tagged your bag and will walk you through security to the gate." But it was 5:55 and Heathrow was a large airport.

Donnie and the agent rushed to the boarding gate. "The last one to board. Here's his bag," she announced. But another guardian angel stepped up, this time disguised as a Heathrow security policeman.

"Bad news. This passenger can't board. We just closed the baggage compartment due to a security precaution. Ten minutes earlier would have made it for him."

Donnie's previously calm demeanor now showed irritation. Noticing this visible change, the Pan Am agent said, "Airman, I feel some responsibility for getting you home for Christmas. If memory serves me, there is a direct Continental flight from Heathrow to Houston. Assuming there are seats available, Pan Am will cover any difference in cost."

Donnie calmed while the agent worked out the details. "You're in luck," she beamed moments later. "Our flight stops at New York's JFK Airport, then connects with another Pan Am flight to Houston. The Continental flight departs two hours later than Pan Am Flight 103, but you'll get into

Houston only forty-five minutes later than our Pan Am connection. Plus, you won't need to change planes."

The agent handed Donnie his new boarding pass with a cheerful "Merry Christmas," then thoughtfully asked, "Can you get word to your Houston friend?"

"No, but I am sure he will be waiting. We'll find each other. Thank you so much. Merry Christmas."

Donnie walked to the Continental boarding gate and relaxed for the first time in four hours. He knew Bill would wait; his friend would never consider leaving Houston Hobby without him.

Meanwhile, Bill arrived at Hobby Airport well before Donnie was due and headed to the Pan Am baggage claim. Within minutes, the horrible news spread throughout the airport: contact with Pan Am Flight 103, from London to New York, had been lost less than an hour out of Heathrow, somewhere over Scotland.

Bill remembered Donnie saying he was taking Pan Am 103 to New York, then a connecting flight to Houston.

Bill watched every TV monitor he could find and frequently questioned Pan Am officials, desperately looking for answers that didn't come. The only information Bill gathered were the ominous words, "Contact with Pan Am Flight 103 was lost less than an hour into the flight, somewhere over Scotland." And the less than comforting assurance, "We will let everyone know just as soon as we hear something."

Two tortuous hours passed for Bill in the Houston airport as he wondered what happened to Donnie and feared the worst. His anxiety accompanied an occasional shiver and muted sobs. Bill paced and clung to the hope that somehow a dreadful mistake had been made. He bought a fountain drink but didn't drink it. For the first time in his life, he experienced total helplessness.

Unaware of the tragedy, Donnie calmly walked off the Continental flight and through customs. As he approached baggage claim, he looked for Bill's familiar face in the crowd.

When their eyes met, Bill dropped the full coke on the floor and cried, "You're not supposed to be here. I'm looking at a ghost!"

"You don't look so good yourself, Bill! What in the world is wrong with you?"

When Bill told Donnie the horrible news, his face turned ashen. His body began to tremble, and tears filled his eyes.

His thoughts raced back to Heathrow, the kind agent, the security guard, and how close he came to boarding Pan Am Flight 103. The security guard's words, "You won't be able to board this flight"—and his last comment— "If you had been ten minutes earlier ..." now haunted his mind. Donnie struggled to compose himself as he considered that possibility.

On the way home, Bill and Donnie shared a reunion of silence and somber reflection as they considered the fate of the 259 people aboard Flight 103.

It took a few days for Donnie to relax and enjoy the holidays. Questions with no answers flooded through his thoughts: *Why me? Why was I spared? Why these events in my life now?*

Donnie called the air force base in London to inform them of the details. After telling his master sergeant, he heard only silence. Finally, the sergeant said, "Count your blessings, airman, it wasn't your time."

Donnie and Bill spent a relaxing thirty days together, but amid the good times they couldn't help but think about the ten minutes that meant the difference between life and death.

On the trip back to England, Donnie reflected on his life and concluded, *Life is precious! God has surely saved me for a reason, and I need to seek His deeper purpose for my life going forth.*

POW

> When you do good and suffer, if you take it patiently, this is
> commendable before God. (I Peter 2:20b)

The hard kick to my shoulder was an unexpected wake up call. But the
hay fork on my throat frightened me far more. I had been running for three
days;—trying to evade capture and return to base. I was ravenously hungry,
thirsty, and exhausted. The German farmer who "greeted" me spoke no
English and didn't need to. His pitchfork spoke volumes.

In 1944, the US and her allies decided to win the war in Germany
before heading to Japan. I was one of four gunners on a ten-person crew for
the large, four-engine B-17, also called "the flying fortress." A gunner's job
was simple and dangerous: operate a Browning automatic machine gun. I
sat in a ball turret below the airplane's lower exterior and shot anything in
the air or on the ground that threatened the bomber during its missions
over German military and industrial targets. We were "softening up"
Germany for Operation Neptune, the invasion that began at Normandy
Beach on D-Day, June 6, 1944.

At the age of twenty, I was drafted into the army air corps. Eighteen
months later, and promoted to E-5, my duty station was the B-17's ball
turret. I sat cross legged with heavy socks but no shoes (simply for comfort).
Fortunately, I had stuffed a brand-new pair of "Evershine" shoes in my
flight bag, bought before flight departure on that fateful day.

Our B-17 received intense anti-aircraft fire returning from our mission,
disabling two of our four engines, and seriously damaging a third. Our
pilots were struggling to reach home base, but the airplane was quickly
losing altitude, which led to the ominous command: "Prepare to evacuate."
The entire crew hastily donned parachutes and jumped into German
territory nearly ten miles from the runway. I grabbed my flight bag and
jumped into German air, hitting the ground in my socks. Our crew tried
to stay together, an increasingly difficult goal. By nightfall of the first day,
we were separated. I was on my own, frightened and running. After what

seemed like an eternity, I happened upon a barn and decided to take refuge there for the night.

Before long, a party of German soldiers arrived at the farmer's barn and added their unique style of greeting to the farmer's hospitality—they roughed me up. Then they transported me to a different location where I was beaten horribly, given nothing to eat or drink, and tossed into a dingy cell. The next morning, every part of my body ached. I was beaten three more times before I received any food—a German version of oatmeal mush. Six days had gone by since jumping from the B17.

After numerous beatings, enemy "interrogators" realized I knew little of strategic importance and moved me to a small cell with other American POWs. The dungeon was a hell hole with no furnishings or conveniences. We could only gaze at the walls surrounding us. However, the company of other prisoners was a welcome change which helped me cope with captivity.

From that point on, my daily routine consisted of exercising occasionally, reading whatever I had available, writing, drawing, conversing with other POWs, and trying to avoid a mental breakdown. To make matters worse, we were always hungry. But my faith in God and memorized Scripture helped me cope with my circumstances.

Although I survived, I never fully mastered how to exist on one meal a day without always feeling hungry or how to live in such unsanitary conditions. Frankly, the environment was almost unbearable the entire time.

After a few weeks, my captors allowed me to bathe and write letters to my family. An eternity later, I received a letter in return. I read and reread the letter at least twenty times the first day and had the letter memorized within two days.

Then care packages with soap, writing essentials, and other "goodies" began arriving every few weeks. The guards opened all of them and ate some of the goodies sent from home. The remaining portions passed on to me were a godsend. I always divided the cookies and shared them with fellow captives to make the joy last as long as possible. I also shared paper and pencils to write letters and to draw pictures of family and familiar places—a real source of encouragement.

This was my life for nearly a year. Eleven and a half months after entering POW captivity as a guest of the German government, my release (and that of my American buddies) occurred through the heroic efforts of the Allied forces. I walked out of captivity wearing the same pants, shirt, and shoes I had on the day of my capture. I had lost almost fifty pounds with the remaining one hundred and fifteen pounds stretched over my five foot, nine-inch frame.

✶✶✶✶✶★✶★★✶✶✶✶✶

Si was a gentle, quiet man. His reputation instantly suggests, "The Greatest Generation." I never saw any signs of bitterness in him. He was a man of faith and active in his church. As for the remainder of Si's crew, they evaded capture and safely made it back to base.

About the B-17: The "flying fortress" was a heavy bomber which was used for daylight bombing runs. She carried a ten-person crew who became family both in the air and on the ground. The B-17 crew consisted of a pilot, co-pilot, navigator, bombardier, engineer, radio operator, and four or more gunners (who operated Browning machine guns). The B-17 became a highly effective war machine and was instrumental in the ultimate success of Operations Overlord and Neptune and the eventual victory in the German theater.

THE FORCE

God is our refuge and strength, a very present help in trouble.
(Psalms 46:1b)

Sometimes, experiences in life are undeniably influenced by a divine presence. This story presents such an occurrence.

In a mountainous region of Afghanistan near the border of Pakistan, this army combat engineer explosives expert was assigned to recognize and disable devices of death and destruction used to harm US forces. Many of my buddies would describe the end of a successful mission with the words: *By the grace of God.* Some would make it out; others did not. My name is Albert. This is my story.

My first mission was to accompany the unit in an eight-vehicle, resupply convoy, driving an enormous MRAP (Mine Resistant Ambush Protected) vehicle the size of a school bus which could take explosive rounds without being destroyed. We were to head north from the gate of our forward operating base (FOB) to a nearby small town. During mission pre-brief, I watched our Afghan interpreter, an amiable, dark-skinned fellow. At one point, I'm telling you, the dude turned white and said, "I don't wanna go. Lots of ba-aad men up there." His spontaneous reaction was a vivid clue that my thirteen-month assignment would be more eventful than I had hoped.

That afternoon, the convoy headed north on a small dirt road only wide enough to fit two Toyota Corollas side by side. I was leading the convoy, driving the MRAP while watching the tedious progress of the other vehicles. Each one filled the entire width of the road. Two thoughts came into my mind. *War is real.* And then the sobering reality, *I signed up for this.*

We continued down the road until the MRAP came to a metal bridge. Protocol called for a gun truck, equipped with sensitive mine detection capability, to cross bridges first. I watched the gun truck carrying my four buddies proceed cautiously onto the bridge, and then explode. My heart sank. *I volunteered for this*—the thought would not leave my mind.

The unexpected explosion threw the gun truck onto its side and blew three of the truck's four hundred-pound tires completely off the vehicle. Looking at the damaged vehicle, I burned with anger toward the enemy. Miraculously, I saw my four buddies walk away with only minor injuries.

James, ever the optimist and convoy wrecker driver, came over the radio, "We still have one working tire on the gun truck." Between us, we decided to hook the wrecker to the front of the one-wheeled truck and then hook another vehicle to its rear. James said, "I believe I can tow both of them back to base." And he did! Using only infrared lighting and night vision goggles, we traveled at a very slow speed of three to five miles per hour. We held our breath, expecting another explosion, but God watched over us and we arrived back at base around one a.m. without further complications.

While on another mission, an explosion took out my vehicle. This time we started on a paved road with the two MRAPs on the dirt shoulder and the gun truck on the middle, paved area, providing full mine detection coverage at about 10 mph. When we ran out of paved roadway, the gun truck switched positions with the MRAP. On this mission, a chaplain accompanied us, creating additional concern for his safety. No soldier wanted a chaplain wounded on their watch. We drove along for six or seven miles without incident. Tension increased. At around four thirty in the morning, we approached the metal bridge where the gun truck had blown up. We followed the same protocol before crossing, anxiously expecting another explosion. Thankfully, nothing happened. We proceeded two more miles before I pulled over to let the gun truck lead. I breathed a sigh of relief.

The gun truck passed, and I moved the MRAP back into formation. Suddenly, I heard a distinctive "ping" in my vehicle. I knew I had hit a buried mine. Before the word "Halt!" came rushing from my mouth, a massive black cloud surrounded the vehicle. Blue chunks of debris, which looked like foam, surrounded me. The pavement below me exploded. Flying debris covered me causing total darkness. The reality caught in my throat—*my vehicle just got blown up*! The melting stench of asphalt and the thunderous concussion hit my body.

The radio blared with the voice of our lieutenant yelling, "Are you okay? Are you okay?"

I hit the radio button and responded, "I think so."

He seemed relieved, "Good. We tried calling you several times."

The blast and concussion wave lasted approximately one minute and created a massive crater in the ground. The MRAP was lying sideways. One of my buddies shouted through the radio, "Can you get your vehicle to function? We need to move?" I hit the start button, the massive machine fired up but was unable to move from the crater. I popped the hatch, got out, and walked around the MRAP. I was in the middle of the road when he shouted, "Dude, what are you doing? There may be other IEDs buried here." They pulled me off the road and forced me into another vehicle for a medic to examine me.

"I've got an enormous headache," I told him. "Everything hurts! Lights hurt, noises hurt, smells hurt." I had never experienced pain like that in my life. I knew something was terribly wrong.

They put me on a spine board, called a medivac chopper, and evacuated me. I didn't go on another mission for at least a month. That was the longest period of my entire tour, sitting and doing nothing until the doctor cleared me for duty. Thinking back, I know I survived the explosion with God leading me and by the quick reactions of my fellow GIs. There is nothing more powerful than the brotherhood between GIs, particularly in combat.

But it was a third incident in Afghanistan for which there's no doubt divine intervention was at work. In fact, the Lord saved my life and those of my friends.

Generally, a convoy trip through the KG Pass, short for Khost-Gardez in Afghanistan's Suleiman Mountains, goes south from the FOB and proceeds up the side of a mountain, about two miles. On this mission, several MRAPs, gun trucks, semi-trucks, and a wrecker loaded with supplies and gear headed up the KG Pass. A gun truck led, followed by my MRAP, to another metal bridge. In an instant, the gun truck in front of me was gone, enveloped in a giant cloud of black smoke and debris. I hit the radio and yelled, "Halt!" On my right, I saw nothing but a mountain. I looked left, and what I saw terrified me!

A metal football in a perfect spiral headed straight towards us from a hundred yards out. Smoke trailed from the football's back end. I hit the radio and yelled "RPG! RPG!" (Rocket Propelled Grenade). Suddenly an "unknown force" came from nowhere and swatted the football into the paved roadway just before it reached my vehicle. The device lay there burning. I looked left again. More footballs headed straight towards me! Same results, the rockets curved to the ground at a 90-degree angle. Six of them hit the roadway. Number seven went behind my vehicle. Numbers eight and nine went under the MRAP.

A buddy yelled through the radio, "Albert, get out of there. We've got to get this convoy moving! Follow my laser if you can't see." He guided me as I cut right and moved forward a few yards. "You'll have a straight shot around the truck that's down." I gunned the vehicle and cleared the immediate area. Suddenly, I heard an explosion behind me, and then enemy fire in front of me. We were in a staged ambush.

After eventually clearing the "kill zone," James said, "Albert, you've got a big hole in one of your tires."

"How?" I asked, "These tires are made to take a hit and keep going."

"I don't know," James responded, "but there is a hole in the tire as big as my head. We have to change that tire."

"Great, in the middle of a firefight and we need to change a four hundred-pound tire none of us can lift. Bring the wrecker and boom up beside my vehicle. It might give us some protection from the gunfire."

James worked wonders. He got the spare off with the boom, lowered it into position, removed the blown tire from the MRAP, and then put the new tire on while several of us, aided by aerial fire support, suppressed the enemy fire and escaped the KG Pass.

He said to me later, "Were you ever fortunate! That last RPG hit the exact spot where your head was just seconds earlier. And after you moved the vehicle, the RPG exploded on the mountain beside the road." My friend James, guided by a guardian angel, was the GI who saved my life! I could not believe what had just happened. It was truly astounding how we all made it out of the ambush with only scratches.

While there are several other dangerous instances I could mention, nothing tops the spiral footballs. We survived them all, and our unit came home with only a few injuries—by the grace of God.

THE GENERAL

Judge not that you be not judged. (Matthew 7:1)

Pinned down by blistering machine gun fire near Quoin Loi, Vietnam, our platoon fought for survival as I grabbed the radio to call in fire support.

Our commanding general roared overhead in his helicopter, hurling orders, dominating the net, and making it impossible to put through an urgent plea for artillery support. We simply needed incoming artillery rounds in Charlie's face, not some maniac general trying to direct a firefight from three thousand feet. Before I proceed, let me be brutally honest—combat can make people say and do things they wouldn't dream of in normal circumstances. It did for me at that very moment.

The general hollered, "Why isn't somebody calling in artillery?"

"If you'd get off the (bleeping) net, I would!"

"Roger that!"

The radio operator looked at me and asked, "Do you know who you're talking to, lieutenant?"

"Don't know and frankly, I don't care," I yelled before calling in the much-needed fire support. Within a few minutes, Charlie's machine gun fire mercifully stopped. The imminent danger to twelve American lives had passed.

Later, I evacuated Vietnam due to grenade injuries—some of which I still carry to this day. While in the hospital, a soldier from Bravo came to visit. "Sir," he began, "The general is dead. He and his dog, along with seven others, died in a helicopter crash, downed by North Vietnamese Army (NVA) fire. The General was observing and commanding elements of his units engaged in close fire near the Cambodian border. The official report reads: *heavy anti-aircraft fire brought down helicopter*. Sir, I thought you'd want to know that our Bravo platoon paid heavily to find and retrieve the bodies of the general and the rest of his crew."

My mind raced back to Quoin Loi and that helicopter circling over our battle area. I distinctly recalled seeing two stars on the helicopter. No doubt, those two stars brought serious NVA attention and fire.

Many years have passed, and I have healed from most of my injuries. Time has allowed me to look at the general in a less judgmental light. My healing led me to realize the general did what he believed would help the troops. I also learned he continued actively serving his country until he approached the age of sixty. That alone said a great deal about his dedication, character, and commitment.

While in recovery, I spent some time researching the general's background. His record showed exemplary service during WWII. As a lieutenant colonel, he voluntarily filled a lesser-ranked lieutenant's responsibilities when he led a small reconnaissance team, penetrated enemy lines, then identified and destroyed four German machine gun positions on an occupied hill. This action, connected with my experience at Quoin Loi, caused me to dig even further into his prior service. As I learned more about Lt. Colonel Ware, my admiration grew. He personally led the team that eliminated a total of eleven German machine gun positions and killed a significant number of the enemy. The colonel personally killed five of the enemy. His team lost five members during the entire campaign. Records show he was wounded; however, he refused treatment until the mission was completed.

Lt. Colonel Keith Ware received the Congressional Medal of Honor for heroic actions. It was no surprise to learn he was promoted to general officer and continued to serve, even twenty years later, in Vietnam. He had a heart for his soldiers, and I came to understand that included even me.

He could have been on endless speaking tours making millions of dollars but chose to continue serving on a God-forsaken hill near Quoin Loi, Vietnam. I now realize the general saw the danger we faced and tried to help my team do the very same thing he'd done years earlier and was doing again when he died in that helicopter crash.

General, I forgive you. Please find it in your heart to forgive me.

About the lead character of this story: John was in the middle of seminary, preparing for the priesthood, when he agreed to a voluntary enlistment in 1966 to become a noncombat clinical psychologist in the Army. At that time, he intended to draw upon his religious training and use it to help with the healing process for wounded personnel. In the reception station, he tested high on leadership test scores and was offered an Officer Candidate School appointment. His training led him to realize he could certainly lead others in combat, prompting his decision to become an Infantry Officer. His favorite expression to soldiers in his command: "I am here to lead and get each of you home alive!"

THE FEELING

Don's Story

The angel of the Lord encamps all around those who fear him, and delivers them. (Psalm 34:7)

Time flew by as Don flipped through an album his daughter had prepared for him and reminisced over various mementos and pictures. At ninety-three, his memory of service as a US Navy pilot remained vivid.

✦✦✦✦✦✦✦✦✦✦✦✦✦✦✦✦✦✦

In my teens, I became interested in building model airplanes, competed in various contests, and won a number of them. As a result, Langley Field offered me a job to work at NACA, the National Committee on Aeronautics. Today, it's known as NASA. I worked in the propeller shop as an apprentice, building giant wind tunnel propellers. It was 1941, and the Americans were preparing for a future where aeronautics would be a pivotal contributor to US defense. Everyone could hear the drums of war coming and the possibility of future US involvement.

I hadn't finished high school when NACA came my way and offered a career that would define my future. It's hard to describe how excited I felt to have a job in my specific field of interest at only seventeen years old. I lived in a rented house with seven model builders like myself. Some of these people became leading pioneers in the evolution of NASA, like Hewitt Phillips, a roommate and personal acquaintance at NACA who later became a crucial figure in the US Apollo Program.

It's amazing how people come into our lives at just the right time and speak truth that gives our life direction. One such person was Zibikowski, a large Polish guy I helped in the wind tunnels. One day, in the middle of working, he looked up at me and said, "Son, why don't you go back to school and get out of here? You'll end up being just like me if you don't!" Since my dream was to become a navy pilot, I quit my job, went back to Roanoke, and finished high school.

By then, the attack on Pearl Harbor had propelled the US into war. So, I went to the navy to enlist. I gave the two men in the recruiting office my background information. The first man asked, "Do you have two years of college?"

"No."

"We only accept applicants with two years of college," he responded.

Registering my disappointment, the second man said, "Come here, son. I am going to do you a favor. You keep your mouth shut, and I'm going to write you orders to go to Washington and take the navy flight test. When you get to Washington, tell them, 'I'm here to take the test.'" He was the second person to give me life-defining direction.

The man cut the orders, and I went to Washington to take the test. That's how the navy gave me—a high school graduate and barely eighteen—the prequalification test for pilot training.

I passed.

After the test, I received orders to head to the University of Georgia in Athens for my training. The course combined officer candidate school (OCS) and basic training, mixing a terrific academic program with a very demanding physical program. One aspect of the program that proved very challenging for my relatively small frame was boxing, particularly with All American football players such as Butch Kissel from Boston College. During the sparring, I broke one of the smaller bones in my leg.

When the time arrived for my class to graduate and head to flight training, my leg had still not healed from the broken bone.

"The navy is not going to send you on until your leg has healed," the doctor told me. "They want you to stay and repeat the course. Besides, you didn't even finish the last few weeks of training."

Again, I was disappointed.

"Where are you from son?" the doctor asked.

"Roanoke, Virginia."

"You are? I'm from Roanoke! Who's your father?"

"Roy Pollard."

"He's your father?"

"Yes, sir."

"Your dad owned a business in Roanoke," the doctor recalled. The ensuing conversation led that doctor to become the third person to speak truth to me and give my life direction. He said, "Go back to your quarters and pack your bags. You are going with your class to flight training."

I went to Pensacola, took flight training in Grandview, Texas, and graduated from the six months of navy flight training with my class. After ten months of OCS and navy flight training, I became a certified navy pilot, an ensign, at the age of eighteen. Born March 23, 1924, I thought I was the youngest navy pilot in World War II, but I later learned George H. W. Bush—also a navy pilot—was born on June 10, 1924.

Over the five years I spent on active duty and the twenty-two years in the Naval Reserve, I experienced several incidents of divine protection. The first incident occurred in flight school. My roommate and I were taking the last of our flight training, all during nighttime hours. No lights, radios, or any other devices were permitted. This was to simulate battle conditions. My roommate came in first, and the signal officer gave him a red light, a wave off. I got a white light, meaning go down and stay down. I landed and had taxied three-fourths way down the runway, and into a roll out lane, when I heard something beating on my wing. Looking in the direction of the noise, I saw a crewman pounding on the right wing of my airplane and yelling words I could not understand. I shouted, "What in heaven's name is going on?" Before he could answer me, another airplane ran right into the back of my aircraft and chewed up the fuselage. The airplane's propeller cut off my rollover bar, causing the tip of the propeller to come within inches of my head! God surely protected me from a painful death.

In came another airplane. With no lights in the dark, he crashed into the two of us. A total of seven planes piled up in a heap because the landing signal officer had not been paying attention in the tower. Amazingly and divinely, there were no casualties.

We completed flight training on schedule. Larry Pencewick, my roommate, and I headed to the administrative office to pick up orders when he noticed a little 3x5 card on a bulletin board that read: "Wanted: Two volunteers for NAS (Naval Air Station) New York."

Larry said, "Don, look at this. Maybe I can get home for a few days. Let's volunteer." I agreed and thought, *He might be going up there to see how to get assigned to a carrier.*

Upon reporting, we learned this was an Air Delivery Unit (ADU). Initially, we moved new aircraft from an assembly factory in Connecticut to a prepping station in New York. After flight checks, we flew the new planes to their assigned base—San Diego, Alameda, or somewhere on the West Coast—and loaded them onto carriers.

While working with the ADU, one of my friends checked in one day and received an airplane completely unfamiliar to him. He said to the dispatcher, "Do you have anyone to check out this plane?"

The operations guy handed him the log book and pointed to the wings on his uniform and asked, "Don't those wings on your lapel signify that you're a pilot?" After an affirmative nod from my friend came this comment, "Then take this plane to San Diego."

Before the war ended, I flew pretty much every type of aircraft the US had available. But there was never enough time to study the extensive handbooks drafted for each plane. Personally, I committed to memory the pilot's checklist: trim, mixture, prop, flaps, gills, gear, emergency fuel pump, carburetor air, wing fold, supercharger, and tail wheel lock. I memorized these basic details and learned to survive, regardless of the type of aircraft. God's providence certainly aided in flying those planes—as it did in other situations. We were certified pilots, the country we loved was at war, so we did what we could to serve. God took care of the rest.

I once had a torpedo bomber catch on fire over Arkansas while two passengers were in the lower portion of the aircraft. When your plane catches fire while in the air, you don't look for the nearest airport, you get the heck out! It could blow up in minutes. I told the two passengers to put on parachutes and get out quickly. One fellow froze in the door. So, the other fellow kicked his butt out the door! By the grace of God, we all landed safely in the trees. I received a letter of commendation from the lieutenant governor of Arkansas for saving two lives.

Another incident involved an F4U Corsair, manufactured in the Vought-Chance factory in Stratford, Connecticut. There were thirty similar planes parked on the ramp waiting for transport when I took off from the runway. I reached 250-300 feet in the air when the engine blew up. In searching for somewhere to land, I feared crashing into those thirty parked planes. I made a "turn off" into part of an open field beside the runway. However, the airplane had poor stall characteristics, causing a loss of airspeed in its turn. The plane cartwheeled, which tore its wings and tail off, then skidded along backward. When the crash crew came and lifted the airplane to get me out, they had to cut my uniform off, yet I was uninjured. God used an armored plate to bend around my body for protection. No other explanation, except His divine intervention, could explain how the shape of that plate turned just enough to save my life.

One more incident made me marvel at how God intervened to protect me for future service. My mission was to fly a damaged aircraft that had been brought back from combat to Norman, Oklahoma—the location where aircraft mechanics trained. In Norman, a military transport was waiting for twenty pilots to board. When I looked at the two military pilots responsible for this carrier, a feeling (like a divine conviction) came over me which I cannot explain. I decided to go to Oklahoma City and take a commercial flight home to Jacksonville Beach, Florida.

When my dear wife saw me, she cried, "I am so glad to see you! Some friends came by the house and told me you might be on the military transport that crashed in Oklahoma. The military plane took off, hit the only high ground in Oklahoma, and crashed killing all twenty-three pilots aboard."

✶✶✶✶✶✦★✦★✦✶✶✶✶✶

Don met his wife in Oakland, California, while on active duty with the navy. He lost her on January 2, 2017, after they had been married for over seventy-three years. They came within ten days of celebrating year seventy-four.

THE VOICE

CHRIS'S STORY

For God may speak in one way or in another. (Job 33:14a)

As we pulled up to the turn, a white taxi moved slowly alongside our vehicle, and I knew something was wrong. My life as a cop alerted me; I knew it was the enemy. But my M240 Bravo turret could not be positioned to shoot in the direction of that vehicle. So, I loaded a magazine into my rifle—it stuck. I reached for my pistol thinking, *I may have to kill this guy,* and then I opened fire. I thought about the thirty gallons of gasoline which could explode if a round hit his gas tank. But this was war, so I kept firing.

The suicide car exploded with a significant blast. I was hanging over the side of the turret as shrapnel flew directly at me—a piece hit me in the right arm. Then our vehicle erupted in flames while I was still inside. *There's no way I will ever get the gurney strap off with a dozen grenades strapped around my midsection,* I thought as the heat increased. *I'm trapped!* The only opening was between the radio and driver's seat, a space of only a few inches.

Suddenly, an unexplainable voice spoke clearly to me, "Get out now!" I could hear nothing except this voice, "This trial is not yet over. There is more to come in your life." It mentioned several things I needed to refrain from and seemed like an hour-long conversation which took place in seconds.

I don't recall everything the voice said, nor do I completely understand. But one thing I do know: it happened, and it saved my life.

Seconds later, at the voice's direction, I shoved through that small opening in the vehicle and landed on the burning roadway. My entire body was on fire. But even in the midst of the chaos, fire, and pain, the voice reassured me, "You are not going to die today!"

I was screaming "I'm on fire" when my buddies pulled me thirty to forty yards from the vehicle. They desperately tried to pat the fire out, but our vehicle was still burning and loaded with five hundred pounds of ammunition, grenades, and other explosives. So, they pulled me another fifty to sixty yards from the vehicle. I was *still* on fire. They started stripping the grenades off my burning clothes and slapping out the remaining fire. I began to realize the severity of my wounds. I had severe burns on my arm, mouth, and face—some were third degree burns.

We assessed our situation—in the middle of nowhere—and realized our vulnerability to another attack. We discussed shooting each other to avoid capture. By the grace of God, no insurgents came!

One of the guys put a tourniquet on my right arm—already bleeding profusely. At the time, I didn't know a piece of shrapnel had severed an artery. His quick actions, and my listening to the voice, saved my life.

I took two and a half years to recover after being evacuated from Iraq, and I never went back into combat. If given a choice, I would have gone back to active duty and fought. But I remained at a forward operating base until being sent home. It was hard. I didn't get to finish my tour and felt as if I received the "easy way out" while the rest of the guys still had seven months to serve.

★★★★★★★★★★★★★★

Chris had nearly a pint jar of shrapnel removed from his body. Today, he still has shrapnel in and between several fingers. A piece went through his right arm, another into his right shoulder, one into his lip, and a piece into the right side of his forehead where it still protrudes from under his skin. After his military service, Chris returned to his police job in Virginia, but memories of Iraq remain vivid in his mind—just as they do for many brave warriors serving our country.

THE SAPPER

> Be sober, be vigilant; because your adversary the devil walks about like a roaring lion, seeking whom he may devour. (I Peter 5:8)

Veterans pay a heavy price to defend freedom; sappers pay some of the heaviest costs in any conflict. Trained to recognize and disarm explosives, sappers also clear minefields with specialized equipment and construct or breach trenches filled with explosives. They enjoy enormous respect from fellow troops as "special forces" in recognizing and disabling mines, minefields, and IEDs (Improvised Explosive Devices).

Also trained to fight as infantrymen, most sappers classify as combat engineers whose duty is to help an army move around the battlefield and impede the enemy's movements. However, some classify as truck drivers, field engineers, or even bridge engineers. Regardless of their title or MOS (Military Occupational Specialty) designation, all expect to perform a variety of field activities—from construction to demolition—in support of combat operations.

*******★★★★★★★★★******

I spent most of my fourteen months in Afghanistan as a combat engineer in support of the Fifth Special Forces Group. I made many combat engineer friends along the way. But my expertise was refined as a mine clearance expert.

My field title was Sapper.

I'd love to say my upbringing prepared me for the success I enjoyed in the army. It didn't. Raised in a military family, with a Special Forces Green

Beret as my dad, home was not a happy place. From my early teens to adulthood, life was a mixture of drugs, money, and fearless—yet foolish—behavior.

At thirty years old, I volunteered for the army as a truck driver/mechanic but quickly migrated to infantry. I still had little fear and wanted to be "where the action was."

I always imagined the thrill of being near danger and in outmanned, or seemingly impossible, situations. At first, I found my tour in Afghanistan very exhilarating. Frankly, I enjoyed being on the battlefield. It gave me a rush of excitement. I slept easily with the sounds of gunfire in the distance or small arms fire going over my head. Over time, I learned to "think like the enemy" and be three steps ahead of them. The thrill of the experience drew me to become a sapper, and the army "grandfathered me into the sapper fraternity" as I learned to recognize and dismantle homemade bombs.

My initial training instilled in me the need to be suspicious of the enemy, perhaps even hate some of them and the values they held. Gratefully, actual experience in the field altered those perspectives.

In many respects the army became my lifeline. It made me begin to see people and life as valuable. When I shipped to Afghanistan, I came face to face with an enemy who tried daily to kill me. That enemy did not represent the average Afghani citizens. When I had the chance to engage with everyday Afghanis, I came to love many of them. In the end, this constant threat, the dozens of Army buddies I grew close with, and even some of the Afghanis ultimately saved me.

I don't mean to convey that I acted foolishly or without regard for safety. Quite the contrary. I acquired the keen ability to sense danger, to think like a terrorist when they placed bombs along a roadside, and to conceal a detonating device. My greatest satisfaction came through finding and disarming those devices of death, dismemberment, and destruction.

Insurgents depended on the local population for concealment and cover for their nasty missions. Naturally, an unspoken bond formed between the two groups, irrespective of locals having no inclination toward insurgent activity themselves. This loose bond of mutual trust led the enemy to develop a "signaling system" for locals to discern where IEDs had been planted and thus avoid triggering the devices in daily travels. Over time, I learned that system.

For example, insurgents used stones (several of similar shape and size) placed in an "L" shape with the corner of the "L" pointing toward a nearby culvert, a favorite and expedient location for an IED. The bad guys also placed a triggering device over the IED that caused an explosion when the weight of a vehicle—or even a US soldier—traveled over the buried, concealed bomb. The seven stones were most often placed on the right side of the roadway, seven to eight hundred feet from the buried bomb. Local travelers then knew a bomb lay in the right end of the culvert and simply moved their car to the left side of the road to avoid triggering the concealed bomb. If there was no culvert but the location was "ideal" for a "maximum impact killing zone," insurgents would simply dig under the roadway, place the device, then gently cover it to resemble the original roadway.

Another way they signaled the location of a bomb on a roadway was to write in Arabic on a large stone or building wall, again seven to eight hundred feet before crossing the device. Sometimes they would put small flags or carcasses of dead animals on the right side of the roadway several hundred feet before the bomb-laden area.

Insurgents were patient, resourceful, and persistent for a cause they believed in. They were willing to die for their cause. They hid like a cobra and struck with suicidal vengeance.

They knew the American army was better armed and more capable of dramatically out gunning them. This prompted their subtler ways of "wearing down the mighty 'Satan' until he gives up and goes home." They also counted on the American GI to become inattentive or complacent. Such inattention could get an American soldier killed, or his legs and arms blown off.

I photographed many areas where I had located and neutralized IEDs. Photos of stones, flags, and writings helped train other sappers and troops to never let their attention wane or let their guard down. Just one moment of inattention could get someone killed, blinded, or maimed for life.

On top of all that cheerful news was the constant likelihood of a remote triggering device connected to a small wire. The actual detonating device was planted on a heavily traveled area and often manned by two insurgent troops. One manned a small wire, concealed off the roadway and often watched by a nearby sniper. The insurgent, almost surely a suicide bomber, held the wired device and was trained to pull the detonating wire at the precise time a target vehicle passed. The explosion would cause the insurgent grievous injury or death. Should they lose their nerve, the sniper would shoot them thus triggering the planted bomb. If the suicide bomber did their job, the sniper stood by to use the explosion as a prime opportunity for a "machine gun killing zone" to take out as many injured or wounded American GIs as possible.

I became an expert IED hunter, so keenly adept I could spot a wire connected to an explosive device at night using night vision goggles. In one twenty-four-hour period, I found and disarmed twenty-one IEDs. The emotional toil of that day prompted my sergeant to give me a couple of days off duty.

****

Living in constant tension of an environment where the enemy plots creative ways to kill Americans with hidden explosives takes a heavy toll on the soldier. It sure did to me. I came home wounded and traumatically affected by PTSD, a condition I still wrestle with after seven years. But I am living proof that veterans can overcome their past, and with available treatments, the Lord's help, and the encouragement of others, they can move on with their lives and put the past behind them.

THE SUICIDE BOMBER

Peace I leave with you, my peace I give to you; not as the world
gives do I give to you. Let not your heart be troubled, neither let
it be afraid. (John 14:27)

Despite clear rules of engagement, well-defined protocol, and correctly
implemented compliance, accidents do occasionally happen. Such was the
case of a young boy who met his death in an unavoidable accident during
normal military operations. After his funeral, every American soldier who
passed through his community met visible disgust from the locals, most
of whom were normal working folk with no ties to the situation. In the
minds of the Afghan people living in that community, there was nothing
the American army could do to absolve themselves of responsibility for
the child's death. This father's mind and heart related to their deep, yet
misplaced, grief and anger. While it was painful to watch and experience, I
knew I could do little to make the grief and anger go away, except pray for
their comfort and remain "on guard" for a retribution attack.

Another event relates an encounter with a street vender I met at one of
the roadside bazaars found all over the country. These byways, typical of
Afghanistan shopping districts, sold everything from lamb and fresh fruit
to fake NFL shirts and Rolex watches. One thing was certain: all Afghanis
loved the American dollar and bartered for it.

The army knew such bazaars were invaluable in boosting troop morale.
Thus, to make it easier for GIs to shop, the army occasionally allowed some
carefully screened local Afghan venders to bring the bazaar to the army
compound where they would set up shop—similar to a neighborhood yard
sale. We bought T-shirts, jeans, electronics, and cameras to mail or take

home. In a strange way, the market reminded us of home. And morale did perk up on bazaar day.

I met a local Afghani man wearing a sparkling white robe and a headdress at one of these bazaars. His command of the English language revealed his education. We conversed on a number of occasions during bazaar visits. I had no problem understanding him when he calmly and emphatically told me, "Our people hate ISIS and everything they stand for!" However, I could not help but think to myself, *This dude is a closet insurgent.*

One day, he slaughtered a lamb and invited me to join him and his family for dinner. I accepted his invitation, but because of my reservations, decided to go fully armed. The more we talked, the more I realized how much he knew, furthering my concern about his terrorist connections. "You are an African American man," he stated. "We Afghanis know how African Americans have been persecuted in America and taken advantage of for centuries. There is a kinship between our people and your people because of that." I listened attentively but remained skeptical of his motives. During the meal, he proceeded to reveal some highly sensitive matters to me, turning our casual dinner into an unexpectedly serious discussion.

His fascinating conversation was compelling and logical. He hit all the right points, seemingly to gain some advantage with an American soldier. Despite my military training, I could not bring myself to hate this man. Nevertheless, a gap remained between not hating and fully trusting his words. Before the evening ended, he mentioned Osama Bin Laden saying, "I know where he is." I didn't give that comment, or the location he mentioned, much thought. But it was the very spot where Bin Laden was later captured and killed by the Seal Team Six raid. I never saw the man again. I have no idea what happened to him, or if he was, in fact, a terrorist in sparkling white clothing.

Regardless, my conversations with him schooled me in how to think like a local Muslim, even a Muslim with terrorist leanings. That schooling proved very valuable during the remainder of my tour of duty as I searched for IEDs. The missions became more challenging and even more thrilling. Success was being able to discern between the person you can trust and the one who is lying through the smile on his bearded face.

One of the tensest and most dangerous situations I encountered occurred four months before I left the theater. Our platoon unit of about thirty GIs was stationed at FOB Sarana, twenty miles west of Pakistan's border in the southeast province of Kandahar. We received a distress report that a disabled MRAP (Mine Resistant Ambush Protected) vehicle needed to be retrieved near the mountains on the Afghanistan-Pakistan border. The specially designed MRAP can protect occupants from most land mines or IED explosives. Eight of us from FOB Sharana traveled in four armored Humvees with turrets on the top, allowing a gunner to protect the vehicle in a 360° radius.

Arriving close to dusk, we discovered the disabled MRAP. No one had survived the explosion, and we were arranging the evacuation of remains when I spotted an individual standing on a nearby culvert with wires the size of jumper cables connected to his body and the culvert. I took a picture of him. Clearly, insurgents had set up this "killing zone trap" to get additional troops sent to rescue the vehicle. Our rules of engagement required our lieutenant to gain *clearance* to take out the suicide bomber before he detonated the IED. Amazingly, almost fifteen minutes passed before approval came. Even more amazingly, the suicide bomber *did not detonate the bomb* attached to his body. My eyes also spotted the shiny barrel of a nearby sniper's rifle pointing at us. Permit me to restate the situation: there appeared to be two insurgents, staging a surprise attack on our eight-person rescue group. Yet, neither of them killed us. Clearly the hand of God protected us during that critical time. When our lieutenant received clearance, we took care of both the sniper and the suicide bomber.

I've wondered many times why the suicide bomber and the sniper did not take us out first. Both of them had the opportunity, but for unknown reasons, they both hesitated. My thoughts went back to the guy in white clothes who befriended me at the bazaar. His words made more sense to me now than when he spoke them, "Good Muslims do not hate minority US soldiers. They identify with them." Could my skin color have saved my life or was he just distracting me for another purpose? Or, more amazingly, was a divine hand watching over us? It certainly appeared so.

With the kill zone trap neutralized, our four vehicles surrounded the MRAP's burned-out hull to provide coverage from all directions. We bedded down for the night in staggered two-person teams to guard through the hours of darkness. We waited for daylight to break, giving us the opportunity to inspect the MRAP for explosives and take our lost buddies home.

Something told me not to sleep that night, but I cannot explain what or why. Perhaps more divine guidance? I stayed awake all night, consuming energy bars and coffee, wondering why the suicide bomber and sniper hadn't taken my life.

At 4:30 a.m., waves of US jets passed over us. Then we heard explosion after explosion as the jets struck targets on the other side of the mountain pass. An indescribable, heart-pounding fear consumed me. Only a mountain range stood between our group of eight soldiers, a destroyed MRAP, and the bombing target.

We found out later that the US jets were striking insurgent troops staging on the western Pakistan border, estimated to be several hundred to perhaps a thousand or so strong. From all accounts, they appeared to be planning an attack into Kandahar or the Paktika Province, first hitting the US Forward Operating Base Sharana—housing more than two thousand US troops—then making their way toward the City of Kandahar, population 490,000.

We spent the night mere miles from hundreds of enemy troops easily positioned to find us the next morning as we rescued the MRAP vehicle. They would have killed us, headed west to kill many more US soldiers, and then ravaged a large city of innocent people. Fortunately, by the protective hand of God, we survived to travel back to base and the "bad guys" never made it.

I was wounded several times during my tour in Afghanistan, in both feet and one hip. I refused the Purple Heart. I was bugged that some troops got Purple Hearts for little or nothing when it appeared they did not deserve it. I felt such types of recognition demeaned this great honor.

Since arriving back in the US, I have received multiple operations for the foot and hip damage. While both injuries are much better, the army placed me on disability and mustered me out of the military. I have accepted the fact that some wounds will likely remain for the rest of my life.

One memory of the welcome home ceremony still brings a tear to my eye. I had my belongings, my weapon, and all my gear as I came down the stairway of the plane in full battle attire. My daughter, Dejah, couldn't wait. She broke away from her mother, ran straight towards me, and jumped into my arms. Well, this soldier didn't act very soldierly at that point. I dropped everything and threw my arms around her. My commanding officer reached down and grabbed my weapon and bag for me and stated to those watching, "There is no problem here at all." There wasn't a dry eye in sight.

My biggest continuing need is treatment for PTSD. The VA's treatment has helped, but I am not good at taking the medications they prescribe. My family has helped me immeasurably. My sweet five-year-old daughter, Dejah, wrote to me while deployed. She is ten now and my entire world revolves around her and my devoted wife. They both understand I am sick and need fairly constant medical attention.

Another huge part of my therapy and recovery is Sego, my five-year-old German Shepherd mix. A Virginia State Trooper trained her from a puppy and gave her to me after I returned. She responds to commands in English, German, and Arabic. Why three languages you say? So no one can control her but her master.

I must confess I came home angry and plagued by impulsiveness issues; however, my sweet daughter, Dejah, my dear wife, Tina, and my faithful dog, Sego, have all been godsends to my recovery.

THE MASS CASUALTY EVENT

A Story of Four Reservists

I have shown you in every way, by laboring like this, that you must support the weak. And remember the words of the Lord Jesus, that he said, "It is more blessed to give than to receive." (Acts 20:35)

October 5, 2005, started as a pretty normal day for the combat zone in Iraq. With no mission plans, we slept past five in the morning. My roommate, Chappy, had coffee and pancakes going when suddenly we heard the most awful *BOOM*, a blast so large it shook the massive fort we called home and caused a concussion wave to vibrate through our bodies.

Kevin was checking email when he heard the explosion. He initially thought a tank round had misfired. After all, an Abrams tank group was bunking at the Fort. So, he continued with his email.

None of us knew the Iraqi police had set up a recruiting station at the front entrance to Fort Tal Afar. They set up various checkpoints to screen recruits and even brought in an Iraqi doctor to perform physical exams. Even though they had protection for the recruits and the Fort, someone had mistakenly allowed a suicide bomber inside. He casually strolled to the area where most of the two hundred unsuspecting young Iraqi recruits had gathered and proceeded to detonate his device of death.

While we put on combat gear, our lieutenant ran up to the roof with a machine gun. We prepared to leave when a first sergeant from H Company stopped us saying, "You guys stay in the Fort and help with the wounded. Our guys will take care of security outside."

"Wounded, who's wounded?" We walked outside and looked. People scrambled to the left and right furiously trying to escape the chaos.

At that point, Chappy, an EMT paramedic and Virginia policeman, went running toward the carnage with Faulkner, another medic at his side. My only training consisted of a short EMT course I received in the Air Force. Little did we know this was the extent of medical capability at the Fort standing between life and death for many of those grievously wounded young men. Mere words cannot describe the amount of carnage and suffering that surrounded us.

We raced to the clinic to set up tables for the wounded. Chappy's medical training took over. Hastily, he set up IV stations and gathered critical equipment, bandages, tape, gauze, and any other supplies he could find. One person started the process of laying out black body bags, side by side. At first count, twenty-eight had died from the explosion, including the scumbag bomber who had filled his vest with ball bearings. We found his head, separated from his miserable body, and let it lay in the hot sun until we had treated or evacuated all other casualties.

But the casualties kept coming. Our team treated over fifty in our makeshift clinic during the hours that followed. We treated those who could walk and then sent them on their way and medevaced more than thirty to local hospitals.

We had two objectives: put in an IV and stop any bleeding. I had never put in an IV, but by the end of that eternally long day, I felt like an expert. Several times, the IV came out. After finally getting it to stay in, I would move on to the next guy. Much like the IV, I had to learn how to use a tourniquet, but out of necessity I became passably proficient in tourniquet techniques.

At the time, this was the largest suicide bombing incident to occur in Iraq. Several guys, some of them officers, fell to pieces and couldn't even put on gloves. After three hours, and with no end in sight, I thought, *Is this ever going to end?* Suffering and death surrounded us. My first patient had a sucking chest wound and struggled to breathe. He didn't make it.

As a policeman in America, I had seen tragedy. But nothing—absolutely nothing—prepared me for this. One patient had a hole in his neck the size of a soda can. I struggled to stop his bleeding. All I could do was put a bandage on his neck before loading him on a helicopter and sending him on for more treatment.

We didn't have time to appoint someone to be in charge. No one told us what to do. Everyone just focused on the next victim they saw and worked with them as long as it took. We were simply GIs working with great Iraqis trying to save human lives. Outside, two guys positioned the landing of two helicopters at a time and helped to load the wounded. As the helicopters took off, two more would land. That went on for several hours. When the Blackhawks finally came, we could load eight people at a time.

Another guy with a sucking chest wound started gasping in the act of dying. I reacted by smacking him and yelling, "Come back! Come back! All you got to do is make it for ten more minutes." At least I know he lived to make it to the helicopter.

Finally, an American stepped off a helicopter and announced, "I am the 3rd ACR doctor."

I yelled, "Sir, please get in there. They need you!" Inside the seemingly 125 degree building, everyone was sweaty and bloody, yet they instinctively resorted to their training. We stayed busy doing all we could to save lives.

We loaded eight Blackhawks and sent at least sixty-four people for treatment at various hospitals. We put more than thirty in body bags and then in a cooler awaiting return to their families. And we treated countless "walking wounded."

When the day finally ended, I asked Falkner—who always had an opinion on every subject—"Sergeant, how do you feel about what we just experienced?"

His solemn answer summed up the reaction of all four reservists on the scene. He simply said, "I don't have words to express my feelings right now."

*****★★★★★★★★*****

These four reservists shared how the bombing had affected them afterwards.

The first reservist stated, "I saw so much violence and gore that day—well beyond nightmares and bad dreams. All I wanted to do was go back to my bunk, take a shower, and fall into an exhausted sleep."

Shane said, "When I got home, I was very jittery and loud noises really affected me. Eventually, I became a social worker and left police work. I have learned to get the bad emotions and thoughts out of my mind by sharing them with others. That and my deep, abiding faith in God has helped me to cope."

Another one said, "I experienced some anger. My dear wife told me, 'You need to talk to somebody.' I knew she was right. I needed to learn patience in dealing with life events."

One reservist even shared his experience with PTSD. "I did trauma therapy and got involved with critical incident debriefs within my world as a policeman. I became a police counselor, and it helped me to be able to help others."

SAIPAN

Carlos's Story No. 1

Fear not, for I am with you. (Isaiah 41:10a)

On June 15, 1944—in the misty morning hours—eight thousand Marines left landing supply ships and cautiously waded through the beautiful shallows surrounding the island of Saipan. Daylight broke slowly overhead as the fog lifted and revealed the tranquil beach. Charlie Company's two hundred and thirty-eight young Marines all made it ashore safely within the target time of thirty minutes. At nineteen years old and frightened, I thought, "Where are the Japanese?" Seconds later, all hell broke loose. Intense, dispersing waves of machine-gun fire opened all along the beach from the surrounding hills. "Lord, help me get through this!" I cried out while a young Marine fell dead in the sand beside me. Dead, dying, and grievously wounded Marines fell faster than I could count. When the machine gun fire finally abated, what I saw terrified me even more. Japanese troops suddenly appeared from tunnels previously concealed under the beach, and thousands more streamed from the hills—all of them ready to engage in hand-to-hand combat.

★★★★★★★★★★★★★★★★★★

Key events in life etch into our minds forever: exchanging marriage vows, holding a newborn child, and witnessing a loved one's passing. These things never leave our memory. Two such key events of my life were the bombing of Pearl Harbor and President Roosevelt's radio address to the nation the very next day. "A day that will live in infamy" remains vividly etched in my mind even now, seventy-seven years later.

Along with several friends, I felt the call of patriotic duty and rushed to the recruiting station to sign up for the Navy. But at only seventeen and still in high school, I needed a parent's signature to enter military service.

Mom wavered over the decision to sign. "The Germans are already sinking merchant ships by the dozens, even hundreds in the North Atlantic," she reasoned—despite my pleas to enter the navy. "If you'd like, I will sign for you to join the Marines," she said. That did it for me. Mom picked the Marines and signed my papers on June 12, 1942.

My enlistment papers to enter the Marine Corps revealed I was too young to vote or drink a beer, but old enough to die for my country.

★★★★★★★★★★★★★★★★★★★★

Two years later, I found myself slowly crawling along a Saipan beach and praying, "God, help me through this day!"

Assigned to Charlie Company, we crossed the Pacific from Hawaii in a Landing Supply Transport (LST), which also carried equipment, supplies, and weapons during the fifty-four-day trip. She joined two hundred and ninety-nine fully loaded LSTs carrying Marines and some army troops in the misty, early morning hours. The expansive Western Pacific brimmed with our fleet as we approached the peaceful looking island. Within thirty minutes, eight thousand Marines and our equipment poured from the LSTs dotting the shoreline as we cautiously waded into the shallows of the island's beautiful eastern beaches. The following day, twenty thousand army troops left LSTs and waded ashore on Saipan's southern and western beaches.

Despite the heavy bombardment of Saipan preceding our invasion, an estimated twenty-six thousand Japanese troops waited quietly for us. Many had been on Saipan for over ten years preparing for the Americans to arrive. They filled machine-gun nests and row after row of concrete trenches surrounded by mountains of flesh-piercing barbed wire. With an extensive network of tunnels embedded in the mountains as well as on the beaches, our enemy was well armed, well supplied, and heavily fortified.

In addition to the Japanese troops, twenty-five thousand natives also called Saipan home and resolutely believed the Americans would bring *"horrific, unspeakable, barbaric cruelty"* to their scenic paradise. The Japanese occupiers had spent the prior ten years fortifying the island and brainwashing the natives. This may well explain why so many Saipan residents committed suicide, most by jumping off the island's northeast cliffs. Many stories abound of Saipan families joining arms and jumping together to the rocky shores below. Others were "assisted" by Japanese soldiers who gathered families in groups then detonated shrapnel grenades and bombs in "benevolent" acts of mass suicide.

Saipan's small Pacific island measured twelve miles long by five miles wide. It took the Marines of Charlie Company, others in the 4th Marine Division, and our army friends twenty-five days of "hellish combat" to capture Saipan.

On day one, I cried out to God and begged Him to watch over me. During the remainder of my twenty-five days battling for Saipan, I felt His divine presence telling me what to do next and guiding my actions. I know that is how I made it through alive and uninjured.

Another memorable day occurred nineteen days after arriving on Saipan. On July 4, 1944, while the United States celebrated its 168th year of independence, the remnants of C Company, along with A and B Companies, captured Saipan Hill Number 171. With eleven causalities and five Marines killed, we renamed that bloody knoll "Fourth of July Hill."

After six more days of combat, we secured Saipan. Fifty percent of the men in Charlie Company were either seriously wounded or killed in action. When the battle for Saipan ended, only one hundred and seven of the two hundred and thirty-eight original Charlie members could still walk and fight. "Nothing could be as tough as this. Surely Iwo Jima will be easier," we all thought.

I don't give facts and numbers to impress, but to give a feel for the scope of carnage we witnessed. Every young Marine who died was a beloved son to someone. This was the true cost for freedom. Among the eight thousand original members of the 4th Marine Division who landed on Saipan and later Iwo Jima, 1,076 were killed in action. An additional five thousand were wounded, though some returned to action after treatment. The combined army and Marine casualties on Saipan included 3,426 killed in action and 10,364 wounded.

The twenty-six thousand Japanese casualties on Saipan included five thousand who committed suicide in the largest Banzai attack of the war in the Pacific. The Americans took 921 Japanese as prisoners of war.

IWO JIMA

And we know that all things work together for good to those
who love God, to those who are called according to His purpose.
(Romans 8:28)

Experiencing combat, horrific as it is, involves the conscious killing
of another person. I didn't hate the Japanese soldier; I hated that war and
combat robbed me of my teen years.

The carnage on Saipan was horrific, but Iwo Jima was worse—much
worse! As much as I believed that life was precious, I knew that war
involved "getting the enemy before he got me." In Matthew 24:6, the Bible
teaches that we will hear of wars and rumors of wars, but we should not be
troubled, as all these things must come to pass before the end of the world.
I took no joy and sought no revenge in killing. Trained as a Marine, I only
did what they taught me to do.

I cried out to God often on Iwo Jima repeating the same thing I prayed
on Saipan, "Lord, please guide each step I take." I believe, with all my
heart, God did just that. I felt His abiding presence guiding me each and
every one of the twenty-six days we spent conquering the Japanese on Iwo
Jima.

The island of Iwo Jima measured less than half the size of Saipan, about
three miles long and two miles wide, and was surrounded by volcanic ash
beaches. Twenty thousand Japanese soldiers waited for us in the hills and
under the beach, just like Saipan. Japanese soldiers, as on Saipan, had been
on the island for at least ten years, building miles of tunnels under the
beaches and in the volcanic hills. Japanese snipers and machine gun nests,
surrounded by strands of razor-laden barbed wire, watched as we left the
Landing Supply Transports (LSTs).

A pleasant, balmy Pacific day greeted us as the LSTs approached Iwo Jima. Again, everything seemed quiet and peaceful. The 4th Marines, including a re-staffed Charlie Company, along with the 3rd and 5th Divisions, totaling twenty-five thousand Marines, bore this mission. At 9:02 a.m., we landed on the black, volcanic ash beach where several inches of powdery dust made it hard to walk or crawl.

Despite my cautions of what happened on Saipan, many young Marines walked around saying, "This will be a cakewalk. Nothing's coming at us." Without warning, the pits of hell opened all over the beach. Shrapnel, bullets, and artillery shells came from every direction as Japanese soldiers rose from tunnels under us and thousands more ran toward us from the hills, firing as they ran.

That first day, we moved forward only a hundred yards through unimaginable carnage. One Marine battalion of 925 landed and lost 550 the first day. That same battalion would go on to lose all but eleven of the 925 who came ashore. Progress was slow and bloody. It took two days to go five-hundred yards and a total of twenty-three days to go the full two and a half miles across the island.

Of the twenty thousand Japanese on the island, we killed virtually all of them. My 4th Division killed 8,982 Japanese soldiers. But we lost sixty-seven the first day, fourteen of them from Charlie Company, with many more wounded. In that one day, our battalion received ninety-one replacements with fifty-one of them coming to our Company.

Each of these islands in the middle of the Pacific Ocean represented a potential airstrip for staging and moving men, material, armament, and equipment further west toward the eventual target: the invasion of Japan. Once we secured an island, air operations would begin and B17s and B29s would re-arm and take off for the next island. Unfortunately, the Japanese were highly motivated to stop the US from invading their homeland—at any cost.

Beyond the raw courage and heroism of American Marines, I saw God's divine hand at work in several other instances. On day twenty-four, we aimed at taking Hill 382. Companies A, B, and C were all pinned down, unable to move. We lay there giving and taking fire. Finally, a young sergeant decided to take grenades and a Colt .45 and rush the first two bunkers. He destroyed both but ran out of grenades. After returning for more grenades, he went back to destroy a third and fourth machine gun nest. However, during his attempt to eliminate the 5th bunker, the enemy got him.

The young sergeant, Darrell S. Cole from Flat River, Missouri, was twenty-two years old when he died in service for his brother leathernecks and his country. "Greater love has no one than this, than to lay down one's life for his friends" (John 15:13).

At about the same time Sergeant Cole made his move, Woody Williams took a similar sacrificial action in the 3rd Division. He used a flame thrower and demolition satchel bags to eliminate the first two nests. On his second flame throwing mission, he demolished two more enemy pits. His final act of heroism took out the last machine gun nest.

The day before we headed to Hill 382, Charlie Company lost sixty-seven men. I was promoted to line sergeant and given the responsibility of insuring line continuity as we advanced, verifying everyone had the ammunition they needed for the day's mission as well as adequate water and food.

I knew we needed more ammunition to make it through the night and prepared to head over to the ammo dump for a resupply. When I asked for a volunteer, no one stepped forward. My ammo carrier, Gross, rested in a crater hole and refused to volunteer.

"Gross, you are still a corporal, aren't you?" I asked.

"Yes."

"Do you want to remain a corporal?"

"Yes."

"Well then, let's go."

As we headed to the ammunition resupply, a shrapnel explosion landed right behind us. It struck the crater Gross had just left and killed everyone inside. From that point on, Gross told everyone, "Showalter pulled rank on me and saved my life! He saved my life." But it was God's divine hand on Gross, through me, on that particular day that saved Gross's life and allowed him to leave Iwo Jima alive.

The first B-29 to land on Iwo Jima came before we had secured the air strip and extended it sufficiently to the length needed by the giant airplane. The B-29 would be followed by the P-51 Mustangs. Pilots would sleep in foxholes by night and go on strafing runs on Okinawa by day. The commitment of those pilots and the necessity of the airstrip motivated us to keep going and secure the entire island.

We finished securing Iwo Jima on March 16th. In those twenty-six days, the US lost 6,821 Marines. Several divisions deployed to take Okinawa, but my 4th Division returned to Maui to prepare for the invasion of Japan.

I never told my mother what I faced in combat. In fact, I didn't tell my wife for over forty years of marriage. Mom passed away before I told the story or any part of it for the first time. I arrived home for good on June 6, 1946, and told the story for the first time on July 4, 1995. My wife sat in the congregation along with eight hundred other people one morning when the pastor asked me to give a testimony to the congregation. During that impromptu talk, I wandered into my wartime service. It was the first time my wife heard of my military experiences.

One last thing—while on Iwo Jima, I asked God to guide me safely through combat and as soon as combat ended, to take away my desire to use any weapon. Since I left the Marines in 1946, I have not touched a weapon of any kind to this day. He answered my request; the desire has completely left me.

*******★*★*★******

Today, Woody Williams is ninety-four years old and lives near Huntington, West Virginia. By the providence and mercy of Almighty God, he survived. Woody is a living example of one soldier's willingness to give his life for his fellow man, and a powerful Biblical example of courage and faith.

The Congressional Medal of Honor is reserved for this kind of bravery. There were fourteen Medals of Honor given for service on Iwo Jima. As of the writing of this book, Woody is the last living recipient of this medal who fought at Iwo Jima.

God gets all the credit that I was one of sixteen men—of the original two hundred and thirty-eight in Charlie Company— not wounded when we returned to American soil. At the conclusion of the battle of Iwo Jima, death had claimed ninety-three of our original company and one hundred and twenty-nine had injuries, some severe. By God's grace, I fell in neither of those categories.

PIT OF HELL

In my distress I called upon the Lord, and cried out to my God. He heard my voice from his temple, and my cry came before Him, even to His ears. (Psalms 18:6)

The self-propelled rocket makes a distinctive hissing sound followed by a screech, then a whistle moments before it hits a target. We learned to identify that sound. The resourceful yet determined enemy fashioned sixty and one hundred twenty-millimeter rockets, then used them as mortars to harass our small forward operating base (FOB). Our quick reaction team from the Army's First Infantry Division established three nine-person FOBs. FOB Normandy sat about ten miles north of Samarra, Iraq (and eighty miles from Baghdad). Our specific mission: root out the enemy and engage them before they brought terror and chaos to Samarra's city of 350,000 and Baghdad's 7.8 million people.

We set up two mortar pits to protect FOB Normandy then heard that distinctive, yet ominous sound. Instinctively, we rushed to the concrete bunker for protection, each man jockeying for a safe position. As the last man dove into the bunker, a rocket exploded right behind him. Little did we realize then, but that bunker would be our residence for the next seven terrifying days.

After we fired off a mortar round, we were sitting ducks. We expected return fire from the enemy. Thus, the concrete and steel bunker built near the mortar pit acted as a life preserver for our crew—an essential element of our survival. The bunker had poor ventilation, no lighting, no water, no sanitary facilities, no signal, and no food. Two portable devices provided our only means of communicating with the outside world.

The bunker offered only a temporary place of safety. It was not intended for a long-term stay. When we took cover there, we never expected to be trapped inside for seven straight days, with mortar rounds hitting the bunker around the clock. There is no way to describe the misery we experienced. We had no amenities, only heat and time.

As darkness fell on the first day, I had the bright idea to race the fifty yards back to the FOB and grab some supplies. The moderate distance should have been easy enough to run in the dark.

This terrible idea was akin to taking my life and offering it to the enemy for target practice. After grabbing bottles of water and as much food as I could stuff in my pockets, I ran a zigzag gauntlet back to the bunker, dodging a barrage of rockets and small arms fire the entire distance. By the grace of God, I made the bunker without injury.

The enemy's quick ability to spot any movement outside the bunker and react with near instant rocket fire led us to believe they had a forward observer with night vision goggles watching our every move. They had positioned themselves in a building near a farm house—less than the length of a football field from us—so close we could have yelled to each other. A row of trees gave their position cover, while our bunker sat in an unobstructed, open space.

But military protocol held us trapped. Our rules of engagement specified that US forces would exercise extreme care and avoid firing into a private residence. This policy prevented us from engaging the enemy and hampered our ability to complete the mission. To soldiers in an active combat environment, this perplexing rule of engagement was life threatening. Our lives were in extreme danger, and we didn't know how to defend ourselves. Military rules of engagement require permission from a higher authority before engaging an enemy in combat. Such rules are assigned at a military command level. In this case, authority resided at a much higher level within the administration.

The enemy took advantage of our situation by setting up near a farmhouse. They clearly recognized our dilemma and turned it to their advantage. We couldn't fire on the enemy, but they could fire on us. We also couldn't pack up and move to a different location, since we would immediately draw fire. Like it or not, the only safe place for us was in that miserable, stiflingly hot bunker. Frustration grew as we hunkered down— feeling like prisoners—while the enemy continued firing at us. And fire they did, day and night, nearly every hour, twenty-four hours a day, for seven straight days.

One tank round could have silenced them; however, the enemy planned to kill the nine defenseless US soldiers corralled in a bunker with little hope of escape. Sixty and one hundred twenty-millimeter rounds bombarded us continuously, yet we could not engage them. We frequently asked for permission to return fire, only to receive a "negative" or no response at all.

By the seventh day, our nerves had reached the breaking point. We genuinely feared we would all die in this God-forsaken place. In a moment of absolute desperation, I cried out: "God, this has to end! Please send the clearance for us to defend ourselves." God's answer came within a few minutes: "Permission granted to return fire." We immediately proceeded to take out the two shooters near the farmhouse. Shortly afterwards, our buddies with the big tank guns arrived and reduced their hide-out to rubble in a matter of seconds.

Walking around the FOB the next day, I could not help but gaze at the bunker, and the remains of the building previously occupied by the enemy. A flood of emotions overwhelmed me as I recalled the horrors experienced in that bunker and realized how close I came to dying.

★★★★★★★✯★✯★★★★★★★

This was the most terrifying experience during my military service. By the grace of God, no US soldier died in the incident; however, we eliminated the entire group of attackers that day. It took a while for the memories to fade, but the experience gave me a new appreciation for life and a better understanding of how God is always watching over His children.

TORTURE ROOM

PATRICK'S STORY

The Son of Man will send out his angels, and they will gather out of his kingdom all things that offend and those who practice lawlessness and will cast them into the furnace of fire. There will be wailing and gnashing of teeth. (Matthew 13:41-42)

Before I mustered into the army, they checked my aptitude. I must have scored very high or very low. Regardless, the army decided I would serve as a mortar man. That occupational specialty involved complex mathematical calculations, angles, distances, and speeds.

During my fourteen months in Iraq, we lost thirteen guys from our unit. Mere words cannot express the hurt and loss I felt at the loss of two close friends. They were there, and then in an instant, they were gone.

The Lord clearly protected and guided me as our unit tracked down and captured a notorious individual known as "The Tiger of Samarra."

It all began in a "retran" site, where radio signals are retransmitted. We were using a remote-controlled plane called "Raven"—similar to a hobby aircraft made mainly of Styrofoam with a liquid propeller engine and strapped on cameras. This aircraft identified suspected IEDs from the air, thus we could avoid sending GIs into potentially dangerous locations. Raven had a six-foot wingspan and could give decent video coverage of a large area.

Burgess, a GI buddy trained to fly Raven, and I were at the retran area flying Raven when we saw a bad guy with a red and white turban tied with a black band around his head. He bent over beside his vehicle and appeared to be digging—presumably to place an IED in the roadway. The markings on his headband identified him as an authority in the local area and possibly someone high in the insurgent ranks. Actually, he was a sheik.

We lowered Raven for better visibility. He heard us, hopped in his truck, and took off. He drove back to his home as we tracked him with coordinates. Pinpointing his location, we set up a raid. Our unit cordoned off the entire town (about a mile from his home) and moved in block by block. We took overwhelming force with us, but still encountered resistance from the townspeople as they fought and died to protect this man. Burgess and I were on the team that entered his home. When we kicked down the door, everyone dropped their weapons and raised their arms. At the point of capture, this "big deal" local leader proved to be nothing more than a coward. He, and the troops with him, surrendered without a fight.

At first, I didn't recognize the man as a former acquaintance. We cuffed him and placed him in the Bradley for transport to base. But before leaving, we searched his residence, found and retrieved a number of documents, then noticed a room in the back of his compound.

As we entered the room, the repugnant smell of rotting flesh assaulted our nostrils. He had constructed a throne of sorts, a red chair surrounded by four severed human heads, with a camera mounted in front. This room was apparently used as a recording studio for propaganda messages. Morbidly, the room also served as a place for tortures and killings.

Returning to the Bradley, in a daze at what I had just witnessed, I suddenly recalled where I had met our captive. I had previously eaten a meal with him and his wife as his children played in their private pool. While the typical Iraqi lived in small cramped apartments, this man lived in luxury with a private pool in his back yard. We later identified him as the Tiger of Samarra—a notorious, former associate of Saddam Hussein who was responsible for smuggling weapons for Saddam's government. According to news sources, he bore responsibility for the deaths of hundreds—perhaps thousands—some of them American soldiers. Audaciously, he complained about the dust from the road on the trip to Fort Mackenzie. When we arrived at the FOB, the Tiger was placed in a location we had reserved for his type: The Pit (an in-ground holding cell in the base compound). I hope he ended up at the Guantanamo Bay Prison and received the appropriate justice.

The horrors I witnessed were not limited to one man's dungeon. During my fourteen-month tour, I saw a number of bodies on public display: some hung from towers and others hung from overpasses. The chilling message such sights conveyed came through loud and clear. I remember listening to an Iraqi man reveal the location of a large cache of weapons. The next day, his severed head showed up at the front gate of our compound. We found the rest of his body at the rear of the compound. I also witnessed a woman, tied up in the middle of the street, being beaten by children. Seeing such things may help explain some of my PTSD issues.

✦✦✦✦✦✦✦✦✦✦✦✦✦✦✦

It seems like I am stuck in a state of perpetual, heightened awareness. My attention drifts occasionally, and I still have panic attacks. I suppose I fear for myself, although I don't desire to harm myself—or others. The medical care I receive involves pills and more pills. Pills don't seem to be the long-term answer. I feel that sharing my story is beneficial and therapeutic. I enjoy sharing what I experienced, and I want others to benefit as much as possible from hearing about my trials and mistakes. I also want others to get a clear impression of what soldiers experience in combat and the challenges they face.

THE DESERTER

Jesse's Story

> But if anyone does not provide for his own, and especially for
> those of his household, he has denied the faith and is worse than
> an unbeliever. (I Timothy 5:8)

During the eighteen and a half years I served on active duty in the
Army, I only recall two desertion events. This story concerns one of those
rare events where a US soldier, after taking a pledge to "uphold and
defend the Constitution of the United States, against all enemies, foreign
and domestic," apparently and willfully deserts their buddies and their
responsibilities during an active conflict. As I tell this event, I make no
accusations and place no blame. The justice system will likely eventually
take care of that. My motive is express the feelings of ordinary soldiers
during the ordeal.

This well-known deserter and I both served in Afghanistan at Camp
Sahara, roughly three miles from Sahara City in the Paktika Province of
Eastern Afghanistan. There was quite a bit of local tribal influence in this
area and significantly less Afghan government presence. Much of the joint
army-air force activity involved interdiction and disruption of Taliban and
other enemy activity that blend back and forth across the mountainous
border between Afghanistan and Pakistan. These operations were extremely
lethal. Nearly two thousand army and air force members served in this
charming area only a few miles from the border.

One of my principle responsibilities was security in a compound of a
two- to three-mile diameter which included the air force runway and several
hundred Quonset hut-like tents we called our offices and sleeping quarters.
I was also responsible for interviewing and checking security for all Afghan
locals entering the compound. The US government hired many workers

to perform maintenance (carpentry, electrical, janitorial, plumbing) and allowed local merchants to bring in bazaar goods once a week. The local Afghan population loved the US dollar and offered fresh fruits, meats, fake watches, name brand electronics, and clothing items at a bargain price. Security consisted of a pat down, a metal detector scan, and a check of hair and clothing. Every Friday, bazaar day, an estimated fifty merchants would enter and operate in the secure area.

Before I tell about the deserter, let me clarify that I did not serve in the deserter's company or platoon. I also did not sign—nor was I asked to sign—any nondisclosure statement for any investigations that followed the desertion or his later release. All of my knowledge is either personal or from the deserter's trusted acquaintances.

When the deserter actually left, the entire compound knew about it. On a base of two thousand, many of them air force and army, we were pretty familiar with most of the units and personnel. Frankly, this news didn't surprise us. Most of the soldiers who knew him saw him as a misfit who didn't blend well with other GIs. He had the reputation of questioning everything. Some of us believed he showed signs of mental instability, although we couldn't confirm this theory.

One of the soldiers in his unit said the deserter became highly agitated after asking for emergency leave a week or so before he left. When questioned by his superiors regarding the reason and justification for the request, the deserter responded that he needed to take care of some personal issues with his longtime girlfriend. The request was denied, prompting extreme anger from the deserter and words to the effect, "I can just leave whenever I want."

Some of his acquaintances shared how the deserter mailed his personal belongings to his parents just before he left—which seemed to confirm his intent to desert.

The actual desertion occurred on a bazaar day when local Afghan contractors and merchants were leaving the compound. The deserter simply dressed up like a local Afghan male and walked off post. Locals confirmed seeing him in town for two or three days afterwards, scrounging and begging for food. Then he disappeared. A week or so later, I saw a video (apparently from non-US sources), that showed him beaten and in bad shape. A week or two after that, I saw a second video, apparently made under duress, which showed him dressed like a local and praising the insurgent Taliban cause.

US soldiers harbored unspeakable hatred toward him. However, there was also genuine sorrow that he had been captured, particularly within the special forces community. These men had gone on missions in dangerous areas and knew what happened to a captured US soldier. Despite any personal views as to his motive, many felt the deserter was suffering and knew they had to find him and bring him home.

But after his capture, we encountered an increase in mortar attacks in locations not previously spotted. Many of us believed the deserter cooperated with the enemy to provide location and mission information never before shared. There were too many instances of our units on patrol being shelled and mortared to call them "chance strikes." A good many of us were angered all over again that a former US soldier had betrayed his buddies.

Despite our personal views, several missions departed to find the deserter and bring him home. A dozen or so soldiers were injured or killed while searching. Two of my friends, Special Forces Green Berets—the best of the best—lost their lives on one of those rescue missions.

To this day, it still stings to remember how one of our own deserted the brotherhood. Despite the cost, we did the right thing to bring him home. My hope is that he will face justice—as any other American would when accused of wrong doings. I make no accusations of guilt or innocence, but trust the military system for the right outcome.

NEVER FORGET

Blessed are those who mourn, for they shall be comforted.
(Matthew 5:4)

Most of our platoon would say we were in an "indirect fight." We rarely saw the enemy, and even when we received fire during the typical thirteen-month tour of duty in Iraq, it didn't normally end in a fire fight. Most of the action came from mortars, rockets, and IEDs (improvised explosive devices) all hidden from plain view. Such an enemy required us to "always be alert to the unexpected or unseen."

This deadly enemy took the lives of my buddies—Mondo and Dixon—and left scars on many others. My name is George. I served in the Army's 1st Squadron 4th Cavalry Regiment and operated from an FOB (Forward Operating Base) called MacKenzie, about one hundred miles north of Baghdad in an area known as the Sunni Triangle. MacKenzie was situated a few miles from the Tigress River where temperatures during the hottest months rose to one hundred and thirty degrees and could easily burn hands, if not protected by gloves. We nicknamed this area "Mortaritaville" due to the many mortar, rocket, and IED attacks.

FOB MacKenzie, named for a Union Civil War officer, was one of nine FOBs the 4th Infantry Division established. MacKenzie was a small facility with poor living conditions but had room for an Army National Guard unit to help with perimeter guard. It also had a ten-thousand-foot runway and a few guard shacks scattered around the perimeter. Previous units did what they could to make this temporary home more comfortable by installing laptop computers and pool tables. My quarters occupied part of an old metal shipping container measuring ten feet wide by ten feet high by twenty feet long. Three or four of us lived in one of these containers.

Windows, power, air conditioning units, and hot and cold water made our quarters a bit more livable.

Mess hall food was never very tasty. Normally it consisted of something in a package requiring only a pot of boiling water to prepare. Most of the time, I ate MREs (meals ready to eat) and drank the always available, but never cold, bottles of water. While marginally adequate, nothing we had took the place of care packages from home. I received a delicacy in my packages: cans of Campbell's soup.

Despite those amenities, I can honestly say we had some of the worst living conditions among the GIs serving in Iraq. We had four phones available for the beloved calls home. But the more action and combat I participated in, the less I found myself calling home. There was little to say that was positive.

One fateful day in August 2004, we left MacKenzie in a three-Humvee convoy. A 50-caliber machine gun was mounted in the turret on top of my vehicle. Dixon, on his first mission with us, drove the lead vehicle. Our task was simple: clear the roadway, find disturbed or suspicious looking areas and examine them for the presence of IEDs. The plan: move slowly, walk the route, and paint each pothole. To help you understand the power of an IED, the explosion from a typical hand grenade can kill anything in a fifteen-foot radius. While a standard 155 mm howitzer's explosive capability is equivalent to fifty pounds of dynamite, with a kill radius of approximately one hundred and fifty feet, the IED we encountered that day was equivalent to three of these howitzers. To minimize risks, team members walked cautiously on the left and right sides of the roadway with the Humvees following behind and moving very slowly—approximately two miles per hour.

Mondo, along with Dixon, rode in the lead vehicle to man the radios and supply fresh paint to the guys walking the roadway. On his way to get another can of spray paint, he suddenly paused, looked up, and gave me one of his big, goofy—yet charming—smiles. Just then, a massive IED exploded, knocking some of us unconscious for a few seconds and creating a large blast cloud. Realizing that Mondo didn't have the protection of a vehicle during the blast, my eyes desperately searched for him through the settling dust. Then I saw him, lying on the roadway a short distance from the place he'd stood only moments earlier. He was alive and conscious. Doc, our medic, jumped from the back seat and rushed towards Mondo. I yelled to Willie, our driver, to get Doc's bag and go help him. My eyes noticed two guys running away. Firing several bursts and walking closer with each volley, I thought to myself, *Should I kill them?* At that very moment my eyes rested on Mondo. The decision became much easier.

Mondo's severely injured legs were barely attached above the knee. Doc and his helpers started an IV, applied tourniquets to stop the extreme bleeding, and gave him morphine for the pain. While being treated, Mondo inquired about the other members of the team. He neither cried nor complained, despite his own massive injuries. The medivac arrived to pick up Mondo, but because he'd lost so much blood, he died en route to the hospital.

Climbing off my Humvee, I noticed a bloody piece of shrapnel lying on the seat beside me. Confused at first about its source, and worried the blood was my own, I looked around and realized the place where Mondo last stood was between me and the exploded IED. The shrapnel might have killed me, had Mondo not been standing in that exact spot. I placed that piece of shrapnel in my pocket and still carry it to this day.

I asked Chuck, "Where is Dixon?" Porras, from the third vehicle, and I rushed to Dixon's vehicle, and found him sitting unconscious in the driver's seat, with his head laid back. I reached for him and noticed the horrific wound to the upper part of his body. When I pulled him from the Humvee, he landed in my lap. His eyes shot open as he took his last breath. I held his hand and said every Catholic prayer I could remember, begging God to take and care for him. We placed Dixon in a body bag. Something didn't seem right. I pulled the bag to the back of the vehicle and opened it up again. Swiping my fingers across his open eyes I wondered, *In his unconscious state did he feel pain? Could we have saved him, had we found him a few moments sooner?* It's been over twelve years and I still can't stop thinking about Dixon and Mondo.

The only injury I sustained came from a small piece of shrapnel. The army insisted on giving me a Purple Heart. I didn't feel like I deserved this honor, especially after seeing the injuries sustained by the others. Although I count my blessings, I still have a tough time processing all that happened in Iraq that horrible day. I can never forget.

THE GOOD AND THE BAD

RON'S STORY

Many are the afflictions of the righteous, but the Lord delivers him out of them all. (Psalms 34:19)

As Air Force military policemen, we were walking fence security in a volatile region of Southeast Asia when a shot rang out in the night. My partner collapsed, dead from a sniper's bullet to the forehead. Instinctively, I jumped into a ditch and returned fire toward an unseen assailant in the darkness. Total panic engulfed me. *Was the next bullet aimed at my head?* I held my breath waiting for any sound or movement. After what seemed like an eternity, a tense calm returned. Mercifully another bullet never came.

That frightening experience remains in my mind to this day. I don't understand why God's providence allowed me to live while my buddy needlessly died.

My name is Ron. Except for a few incidents, most of my twenty-seven years in the military were filled with good memories. Unfortunately, I can only speak in vague terms since a significant portion of my career involved highly classified projects in extremely dangerous areas. I vowed many years ago to never speak about what I did unless the mission changed, and I remain committed to that pledge.

One area I can discuss is my rewarding service in Nevada's "Area 51"— where research and development on the U2 spy plane occurred. You may recall when a spy plane piloted by Gary Powers was shot down while flying a reconnaissance mission over Russian air space. I was an Airman Military Policeman with that program for several years. When our unit completed its training and prepared to leave for the mission, President Lyndon B. Johnson spoke to our class at CIA HQ, Langley, Virginia. He took the time to congratulate each one of us and share with us briefly. Standing face-to-face with the President of the United States, and having him speak directly to me, was the highlight of my military career.

I had to compete with my peers for selection to a classified and dangerous assignment in Southeast Asia. Although I passed, my best friend did not. Perhaps not passing would have served me better. I lived in a constant state of fear and tension for the entire nine months. I had to remain totally alert to surrounding noises and activities. I recall only two instructions from my mission briefing (other than its highly sensitive nature): "You will protect vital US property, assets, and many talented people during your mission"—and this ominous requirement—"Do whatever you need to do to protect both the people and the property."

I also served in Thailand, Laos, Cambodia, and Vietnam. Most of this work involved search and rescue of downed military aircraft. We flew in a white plane with a Red Cross emblem on it. During the day, most of the local men I served with were work buddies. But at night, they became someone else. I never asked questions; they never volunteered answers.

Another mission involved setting up targets in an aircraft test firing range. Normally, I saw wild animals roaming the range, but on one such occasion, we found the area eerily void of wildlife. Things didn't seem quite right. The animals may well have sensed danger in the area. Feeling a bit uneasy about their absence, our team quickly left. Shortly after our departure, enemy anti-aircraft missiles destroyed the entire range.

In addition to the constant danger of my job, I witnessed the unspeakable torture of innocent people by their own countrymen. Most people think of these Southeast Asian nations as stable governments and friends of the US, but they displayed little regard for the value of human life. For example, I saw a Southeast Asian soldier grab a small boy—maybe nine or ten years old—and force him into the woods where he executed the child using his M16 automatic weapon. The boy's alleged crime—stealing a small transistor radio worth two dollars. I still recall that horrific, sickening image in my mind after forty years.

I remember seeing many orphaned children who lived on the streets, hungry and without clothing. Some of them survived as slaves—serving at their owner's pleasure. Parents sometimes forced their own children into slavery, thereby reducing the food burden and allowing other children in the family to survive. Imagine having to make that choice.

The locals cooked a type of vegetable soup with rice and "monkey meat," made in fifty-gallon drums positioned along the streets. I have eaten monkey, dog, cat, water buffalo, snake, horse meat, and a local delicacy called "hot rice balls." The locals would take what they called rice bugs, crush their heads and bodies, add hot spices, and shape the entire mixture into round rice balls then cook them on a hibachi-type grill. Despite this delicacy being a local favorite, after tasting the hot rice balls, I decided to pass on future offers.

Another highlight of my career was serving on the honor guard for the Pacific Air Force. In that role, I met many generals and high-ranking officials at parades and funerals. We acted as pall bearers for honored guests and dignitaries. I met both President Ford and President Carter during that time—along with numerous heads of state and cabinet officials.

★★★★★★★★★★★★★★★

I look back on my career with fondness and mostly good memories. I never expected to do the many interesting things that came my way. In fact, my career began with a stint in the Naval Air Reserve and I became acquainted with the high caliber of people who serve in each of the US combat branches. Toward the end of my Naval Air Reserve assignment, I inquired about the Air Force. In no time, God opened the door to an Air Force career. I walked through that door and served twenty-four additional years. After military service, I became a deputy sheriff for another fifteen years—just for grins.

AGENT ORANGE

You therefore must endure hardship as a good soldier of Jesus
Christ. (2 Timothy 2:3)

War can scar in ways well beyond physical injury. I never received
any physical combat injuries during my thirteen months in Vietnam,
despite serving as an 11 Bravo Combat Infantryman and participating in
numerous air assault jumps with the "Jumping Mustangs of the 1st Air
Calvary Division." Instead, I returned to my beloved Virginia with citations
and awards from the notoriously difficult Central Highlands, near Pleiku,
Vietnam. I also returned seriously impacted by the war with conditions
and memories that will torment me the rest of my life.

In Vietnam, I knew it was the wrong thing to do, but after being in
the field for a couple of weeks, we sometimes got so tired of C rations,
my buddies and I would find a stream and go fishing with hand grenades.
Guys would build a fire on the river bank while the rest of us threw a
grenade or two in the river. We'd scoop up the fresh fish stunned by the
exploding grenade, clean them, and chow down. During the misery of field
combat, everyone loved the fresh fish buffet, particularly when limited to
"two-a-day" rations due to restrictions on resupply air drops. Fishing was a
great morale booster.

The memories of what I saw and experienced still hurt. But I'd love to
take my wife, Cass, back to Vietnam and let her see where I served. I don't
know if I ever will since I am seventy now. Doctors at the VA Hospital said
the Agent Orange caused my Parkinson's Disease. The tremors and shakes I
cope with daily are slowly worsening and will be with me till I take my last
breath. I vividly remember seeing the jungles sprayed so heavily with the

chemical defoliant, known as Agent Orange, and dripping from overhead tree branches.

Our unit served near An Khe and Plieku, located about a thousand miles north of Ho Chi Minh City (now Saigon). Leeches, mosquitoes, snakes, and centipedes thrived in Vietnam. We used mosquito nets just to sleep. In addition to those critters, bamboo vipers—nasty little poisonous green killers—were abundant everywhere we walked. But the leeches were the most painful of my noncombat injuries. Leeches are little worm-like critters that attach themselves to soft skin under the arm pits and other sensitive areas of one's body, then fill themselves with human blood. They liked to fix their slimy selves to soldiers wading through the slow-moving, brackish waters in the area. We constantly sprayed Army-issued "bug juice" on them, causing the leeches not firmly attached to fall off. However, those buried deep in our flesh proved very painful to remove.

Our unit, the Jumping Mustangs, faced combat frequently. The jungle was so thick, we rarely received regular supplies. Often, we had to make do with what we brought in or found. Back in camp, we pulled guard duty, but were at least able to sleep on a cot in a tent.

A typical mission lasted two to three weeks and involved crossing open areas of rice paddies until we received fire from a hut, a hooch, or from a distance. We would return fire or throw grenades until it stopped. We were constantly chasing Viet Cong (VC) or expecting an ambush. Simply, combat was hell. It created stress and kept soldiers on edge most of the time. My mind retained a library of bad memories from the horrors I saw. The VA psychiatrist helped me cope with those memories and emotional mood swings. Yet, I still suffer from frequent flashbacks and visions of the injured or dead GIs I served with—even after more than five decades.

I caught malaria about halfway through the assignment and was evacuated to the US hospital in Vung Tau. The doctor told me bites from female mosquitoes carried the virus. We lost about twenty guys from malaria and other infections during our thirteen-month tour.

There is no way for a combat veteran to describe the horrors of war without mentally and emotionally reliving the experience. I only speak for myself when I say this is painful to discuss, even after fifty years have passed. Without actually reliving the specifics of combat, the killing, suffering and conscious taking of another human's life, permit me to share one glimpse into the mind and tactics of the deadly enemy we faced in Vietnam. Against the miserable backdrop of living, walking, running, sleeping, and somehow (by God's grace) surviving, in a dense, swampy jungle, try to imagine what it would be like to accidentally step on a concealed "punji pit." The sight of buddies writhing in unimaginable pain from a punji wound in the foot, is still painfully vivid.

Many punji traps were constructed in square or circular holes about two to three feet in diameter and depth. The punji stakes were fashioned from bamboo, and when dried, can be as strong as steel, able to cut human flesh as easily as a sharp knife. Punji traps were then covered by wooden branches and leaves.

A soldier walking or running along a pathway where a punji hole was concealed could easily step on the concealed area. The soldier's weight would strike the hidden punji stick, thus penetrating the soldier's boot, foot, perhaps even their leg, and causing tremendous pain and suffering. The Viet Cong and North Vietnamese soldiers would often fill the pit with human excrement which would putrefy and poison the injured soldier's body.

Many punji stakes were fashioned by women and children.

We occasionally encountered aerial punji boxes, strung in the air and connected to a concealed trip wire. Troops walking through the jungle could easily hit the trip wire, causing the punji box to suddenly fall on them.

Amazingly, I was never injured by gunfire, shrapnel, or a booby trap of poisonous punji stakes. But several friends were injured when they stepped on these stakes planted in the ground, causing wounds to their legs, ankles, and feet. Of course, we watched constantly for these hidden traps and for signals the VC left notifying their own of such snares.

We used two types of grenades. Both involved a typical exploding device which caused shrapnel-like needles to fan out from the explosion and strike in all directions—much like a shotgun. I carried an M-16 rifle, in addition to the grenade launcher. With so much gun fire, I also experienced some hearing loss.

The Vietnam War and Agent Orange scarred my mind and body with mental, emotional, and physical injuries. Despite those challenges, I would volunteer and do everything all over again if my nation called. I'd rather wage war on foreign soil than ever let it come to the US. I have no regrets. I love the freedom we know here in America that much.

WE NEED SOMEONE SMALL

REBECCA'S STORY

These things I have spoken to you, that my joy may remain in
you, and that your joy may be full. (John 15:11)

It all started with a phone call. "Jerry, I have a homeless GI friend,
partially disabled and a combat veteran of Iraq. She is leaving a very bad
situation in South Carolina and looking to make a fresh start. Any chance
you and your wife can help her get on her feet?"

A few days later, we met Rebecca and her son, arriving in a small
U-Haul van containing all of their worldly possessions. Sitting in the
driver's seat, the stress was obvious on her small, diminutive face. She
looked like someone who had experienced more earthly cares than one
should have to endure.

Rebecca had driven all night to save on lodging, so we suggested she
and her son sleep before discussing a plan of action. After resting, Rebecca
sat quietly in our den with the reality of her situation slowly sinking in.
Tears formed in her eyes and ran down her cheeks.

"Don't cry, Rebecca. You're in a good place with caring people who will
help you get on your feet. Tomorrow, we will start at the Rescue Mission
to discuss temporary housing, then we'll head to the Veteran Affairs office.
I have friends in both places who can help you. I'm guessing the VA will
guide your search for a permanent place to live and will also walk you
through the protocol and procedures necessary to receive help as a disabled
veteran. Both the VA hospital and Rescue Mission are terrific."

Rebecca spent seven nights in the Rescue Mission before finding a
two-bedroom duplex apartment. The VA helped her locate housing and
even guided her son as he enrolled in a course to work towards his GED.

When Rebecca finally moved into her new home, she lost the stress lines on her face and began smiling again.

After her physical needs were met, Rebecca told me this story:

I joined the army at the age of thirty-four. Things were not going well in my marriage, and I was staying with a female friend. She decided to join the army and asked me to ride along. When the recruiter finished with my friend, he looked at me and asked, "What about you?" I thought about it for a few moments, then answered, "Sign me up." My family thought I was nuts. Frankly, I wanted a new direction in my life.

I took basic training at Fort Jackson, South Carolina. Except for my initial challenge with running, I enjoyed this phase of military training. Despite being short myself, I was tall enough to look over the head of my drill sergeant, making him seem less intimidating. I qualified as a marksman on the M16 rifle. This reassured me that I could hit a target when necessary. After completing basic, Fort Benning, Georgia, became my next duty station before deploying to Iraq. I entered the 5th Engineers Battalion as a light wheel mechanic, working on Hummers, small vehicles, etc. I became quite proficient in brake systems. My small size allowed me to crawl under vehicles easily and work on hydraulic brakes and lines. I became a mechanic for the heavily mechanized 2nd Platoon, and along with other mechanics, accompanied them on missions which lasted from a few hours to a couple of weeks.

Forward Operating Base Warhorse, located north of Baghdad, was situated in an entirely open area. On my first night in Iraq, I entered a fourteen-person tent, sat on my bunk, looked around, and wondered, "What in the world have I done?" Thankfully, the feeling passed almost as quickly as it came, and I never again doubted for the remainder of my thirteen months in Iraq. There was too much work to worry or reflect on risks. We just accepted that danger lurked everywhere.

While on mission, we remained constantly alert to the dangers presented by UXOs (unexploded ordnances). Every soldier looked for disturbed areas, trip wires, or culverts. During my tour, we found and disabled several UXOs without losing any members of our unit. Yet, the constant pressure unnerved us at times.

One day while heading up an inclined roadway, one of the large vehicles started losing hydraulic fluid. Because this fluid supported its braking and hydraulic lift system, it created a potentially dangerous and disabling situation which could impact our mission success. As the duty mechanic, the sergeant directed me to find and fix the problem. Admittedly tense, I removed my helmet, protective vest and all weaponry (items essential to my ability to defend myself), then crawled under the vehicle to find the problem. Fortunately, other soldiers surrounded the convoy, creating a ring of security. I quickly found and fixed the problem, a loose coupling on the main brake line. I tightened the loose fitting and checked the others. Problem solved. What a relief to put my gear back on, return safely to my vehicle, and resume the mission. By the grace and protective hand of God, no enemy attacked us during the twenty minutes it took to fix the problem.

God's guiding hand saved us from a close call one Sunday afternoon. While on duty seven days a week, the command staff was sensitive to our need for occasional free time. We completed scheduled vehicle maintenance at one in the afternoon, so the command sergeant let our crew take off for the rest of the day. I went back to my tent to do laundry when an enemy round scored a direct hit on the motor pool. We had just left that exact work station minutes earlier—another clear indication of God's protection.

Another incident occurred on a routine patrol. One of the gunners was singing the Smurf song when his vehicle hit a concealed IED and exploded suddenly. Communications went silent. I was looking directly at his vehicle when the explosion occurred. A few moments of anxious silence passed before we heard his dazed voice announcing, "I'm okay." What a blessed relief!

Another unfortunate situation involved one of the sergeants in the motor pool, who tried to commit suicide. Noting several of the comments he made, the captain and other sergeants intervened in time; however, his actions led to his removal and return to the US. We later heard of his final suicide attempt by drowning. This was the saddest news I received during my entire career, especially since everyone in the battalion seemed to like him.

✱✱✱✱✱✱★★★★★✱✱✱✱✱✱

I never received a PTSD diagnosis. But I do suffer from frequent nightmares, whether from the stress of combat or bad times in my childhood and marriage, I really can't say.

I have no regrets regarding my time in the army and am grateful to God for the time I spent there. I would do it all again. As a woman, I feel I had every opportunity to succeed. Perhaps females needed to work harder to earn the respect of the men, but the respect was there, and I am grateful I earned it. I was one of five women soldiers in a platoon and one of sixteen women in a company of one hundred and fifty. I saw many of the guys go out of their way to protect the females, but over time, the women came to understand that genuine respect is earned regardless of gender.

I left the army as an E5, after serving for six years. My disability came from chronic migraines and fibromyalgia. It was not diagnosed upon entering military service, but it gradually worsened during my overseas tour. The actual diagnosis and disability designation came after I returned to Fort Benning.

LIBERTY BRIDGE

Foolishness is bound up in the heart of a child; the rod of correction will drive it far from him. (Proverbs 22:15)

Shane is the perfect example of a Marine's Marine—a "grunt." When asked why he joined the Marine Corps, he laughed and gave this answer:

It all started when I ended up in a West Virginia jail with my childhood friend, Bud. We stood before the judge and heard about the fines we faced, and Bud announced, "Your honor, I'll pay the fines."

The judge looked at him, "You have that kind of money?"

"Yes, sir, in my car," Bud answered. "If you will allow a deputy to take me to my car, I can pay for all the damages and fines. But, Judge, can you tell me where the tow truck took my car?"

After releasing Bud, the judge turned his attention to me, an ornery seventeen-year-old at the time. "Since you're underage, I cannot release you to anyone but your father." Sizing me up, the judge asked, "Have you ever thought about the Marine Corps?"

I had always wanted to be a Marine. So when the judge gave this as a choice, my dad willingly signed the enlistment papers, and I was in the Marine Corps.

I left the West Virginia jail and went straight to Parris Island, South Carolina. The Marine Corps was the best thing that ever happened to me—other than meeting and marrying my wife. It made me realize that no matter how tough I felt, there was always someone out there tougher than me.

On the first day of boot camp, the drill instructor yelled to our platoon, "If any of you thinks you're tough enough to take on Drill Sergeant Carver, step out." I stepped out, and he hit me so hard I thought my life had ended!

By the time we deployed to Vietnam, he had become my first real father figure in the Marine Corps, and I respected him.

But the scariest situation I encountered in my life happened at Liberty Bridge in Vietnam. The bridge sits in Quang Nam Province on the Thu Bon River. Of the fourteen-thousand Marines killed in Vietnam, ten thousand died in Quang Nam Province.

Liberty Bridge—a massive wooden structure—was the longest timber bridge in Vietnam, built by Navy Seabees and completed in July 1968 as a critical way to bring troops, equipment, and supplies to the Marine units. While we set up a firebase at the bridge for security, the enemy developed a nasty, persistent habit of testing that security after dark. Our strategy on this flat location was simple—establish and maintain a presence near the bridge. The enemy, however, was determined to destroy our base. Intermittently, we fired mortars around the perimeter to discourage them from getting too close. All night, we'd watch the green and red tracers of bullets fly into the black sky as we'd wait for the next attack.

By day, our unit ran regular sweeps of the highway between Da Nang and the city of An Hoa—focusing on a twenty-five mile stretch of road. Da Nang is a large coastal city on the South China Sea which lies north of Liberty Bridge; An Hoa lies thirty miles south. We walked back and forth for eight to twelve hours, day after day, sweeping the roadway for mines.

By night, we hunkered back down in the firebase near the southwest end of the bridge in a flat, open area. We knew the enemy surrounded us, all the time, day and night.

The incident I recall so vividly began at 2:30 a.m. I was asleep in one of the three supply bunkers when an alarm sounded. It blared near the gate, growing louder and louder. That piercing noise echoed throughout the camp. Marines awoke, mustered weapons, and ran to the perimeter. I put my flak jacket on, grabbed my rifle, ammunition, grenades, a knife, and ran out too.

The sight my eyes beheld made me want to wet my pants. There were black pajama-clad soldiers everywhere. Even in the darkness, silhouettes of countless black pajamas appeared in every direction around the perimeter of the small Marine outpost! If I had to guess, several hundred (perhaps a battalion-sized unit of four hundred to five hundred) surrounded us, preparing to overrun our firebase. Our company of 132 Marines and Navy Seabees faced an enemy force four times our size.

We were kids fighting against insurmountable odds. I was only eighteen years old, and my legs trembled throughout the battle. Regardless of age or rank, everyone fought. I remember Sgt. Robert E. Pike headed up the chow hall. His mess hall personnel peeled potatoes and washed pots by day. But at this moment, everyone had a weapon in their hands to face an enemy determined to kill us at any cost. I could hardly believe what I saw—mess hall guys fighting and running, fighting and running. These young Marines showed unbelievable bravery. They were running *toward* the black pajamas and firing as they ran.

I thought we would run out of ammo, we fired so much and killed so many. But we couldn't kill them fast enough! As some fell, more took their places and advanced. We kept killing them, and they kept coming, climbing over the bodies of their fallen comrades. An unbelievable sight! In the middle of that horrific event, things happened fast. I knew we were all going to die; it was just a matter of when. The attack continued for at least three hours of non-stop fighting.

The next morning, things settled down, and we started counting the bodies, looking for the wounded and determining who we could save. Gunnery Sergeant Burns, covered in blood, carried the wounded for treatment. He exclaimed, "What a night to remember!" It was a night I will never forget. I can honestly say it was the worst night of my life. I cried at the horrific sights I saw and still tear up at the memories. I never experienced anything even close to that horror for the rest of my time in Vietnam; but, thank the Lord, I survived.

In the daylight, I saw evidence of the enemy's gruesome determination. They had tightly wrapped wire around their legs, so if wounded they could slow the bleeding and keep fighting before dying. Though horrific and frightening, they had come prepared to die. One of the news networks flew over the site the next morning and reported that they couldn't begin to count the bodies in black pajamas stacked on top of each other, covering the fence around the firebase. The newsman somberly summed it up, "As a war news reporter, I have never seen anything like this in my entire life."

For me, the worst moment came when a Marine stumbled over a small dead body. I rolled the body over and remembered knifing him across the throat and chest during the battle. I looked into his face. His dog tag showed he was *thirteen years old*, only a child. The memory of his lifeless eyes haunts me to this day.

I understand war and know what one has to do in war. But when you are personally responsible for taking the life of a kid, snuffing it out, it never leaves you. It still brings tears to my eyes when I think of it. Although I had no children at the time, I would later look at my own son and remember that moment. He was just a kid.

Shane told me his story with tears streaming down his rough, wrinkled face. Even five decades after the event, this man stood before me, weeping, as he relayed the most powerful and vivid memory of his life. After he finished his tour in the Marine Corps, he passed through Manassas, Virginia, where he met Elizabeth, the love of his life. "She is the angel whom God sent to rescue me—the one who came into my life when I needed her the most."

FALLUJAH

Brandon's Story

> To everything there is a season, a time for every purpose under
> heaven: a time to be born, and a time to die … a time to kill,
> and a time to heal; a time to break down, and a time to build up.
> (Ecclesiastes 3:1-2a, 3)

I arrived in Iraq in time to participate in Operation Phantom Fury. The battle lasted for thirty-three days. At the end of the campaign, commanders told us this was the bloodiest battle since the Marines waged war in Hue, Vietnam. That brought a smile of satisfaction since my mentor and example of Marine service came from my dad, Shane, who fought in Hue as a young Marine.

Although the strategy our officers implemented for Fallujah appeared brilliant, it was also slow, time consuming, tortuous, and bloody. Maintaining this strategy throughout the campaign required a determined and dedicated communications plan. Essentially, we assaulted an entire city moving in one contiguous line—one house, one block, and one street at a time. The enemy had no escape. We located the enemy and demanded their surrender.

Street by street and house by house combat proved very difficult—even for Marines—however, we received protection from the army and the air force. The army provided tank and armored vehicles for the assault, and the air force gave us outstanding air cover.

We attacked the city in a deliberate manner by entering every structure. As we sought out the enemy, we took no one (man, woman, or child) and no situation for granted. We had them surrounded; the city was doomed. Slow, but measured, progress put us two blocks into the city within two weeks. This allowed us to set up a field hospital behind our lines. During the last two and a half weeks, the battle became less intense as we progressed.

Before our assault, we dropped pamphlets, written in Arabic, all over the city. We wanted to warn the civilian population of our coming and told them we considered the city a "free-fire zone." We also wanted to convey that we had no defined rules of engagement; thus, citizens should leave while they could. A great many did. Patrol boats covered the rivers within the city. Along one of these rivers, the enemy had hung the bodies of four American contractors on a bridge we called "Blackwater Bridge."

During Operation Phantom Fury, we were required to look out for a reporter traveling with us. This really upset me. He came from a cable television news network. Since he did not always report the truth, it appeared he only wanted to make a name for himself. The Marines who protected him resented how he wrote stories with an inaccurate slant of the facts surrounding our situation. I can say with certainty that none of the Marines trusted him.

When I came home from my first tour in Iraq, I dealt with extreme anger over what I had faced and the horrible things I saw humans doing to other humans. As a way of dealing with my anger, I resorted to drinking heavily and often engaged in fits of rage.

Even after all I'd gone through, I felt the need to do more; therefore, I volunteered for two additional tours in Iraq. Thankfully, neither involved as much combat as the first one.

★★★★★★★★★★★★★★★★★

We ended our time together by looking at pictures of Brandon's fellow Marines. As he looked though the photographs, he stopped on one picture of a young man named Brad. Mist formed in his eyes as he stated, "This was the finest human being I ever met. He didn't drink, didn't smoke, didn't curse, and didn't even engage in premarital sex—just a terrific person. He was very religious and a devout follower of God."

★★★★★★★★★★★★★★★★★

Brad received a promotion to corporal about a week before I did. When we used a vehicle in the patrol, we'd switch back and forth. One of us would handle the gun mounted on the vehicle while the other stayed on the ground. Then for the next patrol we would switch positions. On November 10, 2004, Brad was supposed to be in the vehicle and I on the ground. But on that morning, he came to me and announced, "Brandon, I had a dream last night. I'm supposed to be on the ground again today." After a few back and forth remarks, he pulled rank and flatly stated, "Brandon, you are in the truck today, and I am on the ground!"

I boiled with anger toward him. Every Marine wanted to be on the ground rather than riding in an armored vehicle. Fuming, I jumped into position behind the vehicle's gun.

Less than an hour into our patrol, Brad took three rounds in the chest from an AK-47. The terrific force of the gun punctured his protective vest. He was dead before he hit the ground. To this day, I feel that Brad took the hit meant for me.

After we returned to the States, the whole platoon went to Brad's home. I went to his bedroom and just sat there. I could almost feel his presence. "Brad, why did you make me change places with you? If only you'd listened, you would be here right now instead of me." I cried out as I looked around the room devoid of his presence.

✶✶✶✶✶★★★★★★★✶✶✶✶✶✶

After recounting the gripping details of his time in Iraq, Brandon went on to say, "I was never wounded," and looking upwards he added, "Thank you, Jesus! My scars were mostly emotional ones. The VA diagnosed my condition as PTSD (Post Traumatic Stress Disorder).

"My mother, wanting to help me cope with my anxieties, stayed up with me on several occasions. I knew her constant prayers for my safety, and God's providential care, brought me home without a scratch. Her faith and prayers also helped me deal with the anger.

"I mustered out of the military on thirty percent disability and still receive treatments for PTSD from McGuire Veterans Hospital. They have a wonderful medical staff there. After a lot of bureaucracy, I began receiving a modest disability check because of the PTSD.

"My mom encouraged me to pursue my gift of expression through poetry. This poem was written while in combat, and at a time when my faith was at a very low ebb. I wrote it to honor the fallen heroes with whom I served and gave it the title 'These Courageous Few.'"

I am the calm on all sides,
The raging storm,
This killing and dying has become the norm.
These brave fellows, these courageous few,
Would be rejected by the world if the world only knew,
The things that we in an average day do.
Slowly I see humanity slipping away.
Finally there is nothing, not a thing left to see,
But the beast inside them and the one inside me.
Are we still human, who do inhuman things?
And is that soul whole that no longer sings?
So cry if you will, pray if you can,
For the things done to man by another man.
Do unto others as they do unto you;
But in the end that's as empty as these courageous few.

Lance Corporal Charlie Seaborne,
Fallujah, Iraq 2004

CONCLUSION

Writing this book has been a labor of love. Hearing their stories has opened my eyes to some of the challenges the men and women in the military faced on the battlefield and continue to face to this day. I also have been given a new awareness of the price of freedom. I commend all veterans for their service. They have my deepest respect and admiration.

ABOUT THE AUTHOR

Jerry Barnes has served his country for a total of forty-three years—three years active duty as an Army Combat Engineer, two additional years in the Army Reserve and thirty-eight years as a civilian with the Army Corps of Engineers.

After receiving a bachelor's degree in civil engineering from Virginia Tech, he was commissioned as a second lieutenant in the army. Having completed his tour of active duty, he continued working with the Corps of Engineers as a civilian, retiring as the Director of Operations in 2007. After a year, he returned to work, serving as Special Assistant to the Secretary of the Army.

His passion for honoring the men and women who faithfully serve our country led him to write *When Heaven Visits, Dramatic Accounts of Military Heroes*. In the course of writing this book, he has met many other brave young men and women who have a story to tell. He is currently working on a sequel, *Combat Survivor Heroes*, which should be out in the next few months.

NOTES

✳✳✳✳✳✳★★ ★ ★★✳✳✳✳✳✳

Major General Keith Ware (the general) received the Medal of Honor for personally leading a successful, small-team attack on a heavily fortified German hilltop position on December 26, 1944. He was a lieutenant colonel at the time. General Ware entered the Army as a recruit and worked his way through the enlisted ranks to earn a commission. He was killed in action on September 13, 1968, while leading a combat operation in Vietnam.

GLOSSARY

155 mm Artillery Round—Each round has about 12-15 pounds of dynamite and weighs 43 kg or about 85 pounds. The round has been used extensively by the Army and Marines since the mid-1960s to destroy buildings, equipment and personnel.

50-Caliber Turret—This machine gun is mounted on a metal platform and the gunner is positioned in the middle of the vehicle. Visibility from the turret is for 360-degree firing.

AK-47—A standard automatic weapon used extensively in combat units.

Ball Turret—A small spherical shaped gun (designed to reduce drag) fitted to the bottom, top and sometimes to the nose areas of selected bombers. Most turret gunners had split seconds to fire upon approaching enemy aircraft and were sitting ducks for enemy return fire.

Bradley Fighting Vehicle—This heavily armored vehicle has a crew of three and can transport six fully armed soldiers to and from, or around, the battlefield. It provides protection from small arms fire by the enemy and gives soldiers inside ample protection and visibility. The Bradley's top speed is about thirty-five mph.

Concertina Wire—Continuous strands of heavy gauge wire with razors manufactured into the wire every few inches. Concertina wire is very effective in providing security with visibility. It is difficult for humans to penetrate (pass over or through) this barricade.

Humvee—A standard utility vehicle used extensively in the Army and Marine Corps as a mode of transportation. This vehicle is heavily armored and able to withstand significant explosive power.

LSTs—These Landing Supply Ships (or transports) were built for the Navy during and following WWII. They supported amphibious operations by carrying tanks, vehicles, cargo, and landing troops directly onto shore with no docks or piers. Most LSTs carried a company sized unit of 225+, equipment, food, and fuel across the Pacific, generally from Hawaii. LSTs also had a crew of about 100. They were about 380 feet in length, or a bit longer than a football field. About 1,000 LSTs were built during WWII.

Propeller Driven B-17s and B-24s—These planes were used extensively in WWII for bombing missions in the Pacific and over targets in Europe.

Squirter—A combatant who tried to avoid capture by running.

BIBLIOGRAPHY

The Holy Bible, New King James Version, Thomas Nelson, Inc., Nashville, Atlanta, London, Vancouver, 1992.

Nave's Topical Bible, A Digest of the Holy Scriptures, The Southwestern Company, Nashville, Tennessee, 1962.

All stories in When Heaven Visits were transcribed from recordings, notes, and face or phone discussions with each veteran. Permission to publish each story was granted by the veterans. 2018, 2019.

CPSIA information can be obtained
at www.ICGtesting.com
Printed in the USA
BVHW030221220822
645171BV00011B/437